D1177618

The Muses' Library

★

SELECTED POEMS
OF
WILLIAM BARNES

SELECTED POEMS

OF

WILLIAM BARNES
1800—1886

edited
with an introduction .
by

GEOFFREY GRIGSON

LONDON
ROUTLEDGE AND KEGAN PAUL

First published in 1950
by Routledge & Kegan Paul Ltd.
68 Carter Lane, London E.C.4
Printed in Great Britain
by Latimer, Trend & Co. Ltd
Plymouth

CONTENTS

v

CONTENTS

CONTENTS

CONTENTS

CONTENTS

CONTENTS

x

INTRODUCTION

I

Recollections we have of William Barnes are mainly of him as a middle-aged, old or dying poet. Many of them are in the *Life* written by his daughter, Lucy Baxter—a book, so few were those who admired Barnes, which sold only 267 copies. William Allingham, Locker Lampson, Coventry Patmore, Tennyson, and later on Edmund Gosse and Thomas Hardy, all knew him in this way as the patriarchal clergyman with the long beard.

Gosse and Hardy went to see Barnes not long before his death: 'We found him in bed in his study, his face turned to the window, where the light came streaming in through flowering plants, his brown books on all sides of him save one, the wall behind him being hung with old green tapestry. He had a scarlet bedgown on, a kind of soft biretta of dark red wool on his head, from which his long white hair escaped on to the pillow; his grey beard, grown very long, upon his breast; his complexion, which you recollect ("you" is Coventry Patmore) as richly bronzed, has become blanched by keeping indoors, and is now waxily white where it is not waxily pink; the blue eyes half shut, restless under languid lids . . . I wish,' Gosse went on, 'I could paint for you the strange effect of this old, old man, lying in cardinal scarlet in his white bed. . . .' Palgrave also describes him a year before his death, his 'finely cut face', his 'hands fine like a girl's', adding 'Titian or Tintoret had no nobler, no more highborn looking sitter among the doges of Venice.'

His death came on October 7th, 1886. And on the 11th, as he was carried out, the sun flashed off his

1

coffin to Thomas Hardy as, some fields away, he was walking across to the funeral—to the funeral of the man from whom he had learned the forms of poetry:

> Thus a farewell to me he signalled on his grave-way
> As with a wave of his hand.

William Barnes was eighty-five or eighty-six when he died. There is some doubt whether the year of his birth had been 1800 (as Thomas Hardy believed) or 1801, though certainly he was christened early in 1801. Perhaps because he was small and delicate there may have been some long interval between birth and being taken off to the font. 'I, the son of John and Grace Barnes', his own manuscript *Notes on the Life of William Barnes* begin, 'was born at Rush-hay, a farmling at Bagber in the Parish of Sturminster Newton in the Vale of Blackmore'—and from there on, it is true, we know at least the skeleton of his quiet and isolated life. First there was a Dame school, then a school at Sturminster, and then 'I was taken while yet a boy into the office of Mr. Dashwood, a learned lawyer of Sturminster, and after a while I went into that of Mr. Coombs at Dorchester, and was just then eighteen years old, and very kind to me was Mr. Coombs. . . . I was not unfaithful to my desk, but I daily spent a share of my spare time on the study of those higher branches, Latin and Greek and others, which I had not reached at school, but with my strong love of learning and art I felt that I was not in my right, or most mind-fitting way of life.' A chief event in his childhood in the Vale of Blackmore had been the death of his mother, a chief event in Dorchester his meeting with Julia Miles, whom he married in 1827. He had first seen her climbing down from the coach in High Street, a child of sixteen with blue eyes, wearing a sky-blue 'spencer' or jacket. She was the cause and the centre of his love poems in her life and after her death; from his own boyhood, when he cele-

brated her 'bright azure eyes' in a poem in his first
book printed at Dorchester in 1820, into his old age.

When he married Julia Miles (whose father was in
the excise at Dorchester), Barnes was running his own
school, just outside his native county, at Mere, in
Wiltshire. To his languages he was now adding Italian,
French, German, and Persian. He practised wood-en-
graving—'I had from a love of Art, tried my graver on
wood, quickened moreover by Bewick's works, and it
was a day-dream of my youth that I might follow Art
as my way of life'—wrote for the *Dorset County
Chronicle* and the *Gentleman's Magazine*, concerned
himself with etymology, with playing the flute, the
violin and the piano, and singing and composing. He
kept his diary in Italian; and was visiting Wales, and
exploring Welsh poetry and prosody (long in advance
of Hopkins). And at Mere he began for the first time to
write poems in his native dialect. He had a liking for
archaeology (he gave up the study of Russian, since it
was 'wanting in old lore'). He had a turn for mechani-
cal invention, instrument making, and mathematics. In
fact, through all his pursuits, as through his poetry,
goes a passion for form and reason. There is an excellent formality about his wood engravings, and throughout his life he felt the desire for visual order within a
frame. At twenty-one he had gone so far in his wish to
be a professional engraver and artist that approaches
were made for him to Rudolph Ackermann in London,
but the replies of the art publisher and of the engraver
Edward Scriven were discouraging. He remained an
amateur, and later in his life became ardent in the collection of paintings and engravings.

Barnes left Mere in 1835 and went back to his own
county to open a second school in Dorchester, where
he was 'so lucky, as to have . . . a friend who was a good
Oriental scholar, Col. Besant, theretofore of the native
Bengal infantry, and author of the Persian and Urdu

Letterwriter, with whom for some years I read a little Hindustani or Persian once almost every week'. In 1840 he lost the most intimate of his friends, Edward Fuller, who had shared his taste for art and letters. In 1844 Sheridan's grandson invited Barnes over to Frampton Court, to meet his beautiful sisters, the writers Lady Dufferin and Caroline Norton, who were taken by his dialect poems in the *Dorset County Chronicle*. Barnes at first refused to go 'on the grounds that he was un-accustomed to society', but gave way to another letter, went, and enjoyed himself; and in Mrs. Norton made a friend who was the first and for some years the last well-known writer to give him attention. He was or-dained deacon by the Bishop of Salisbury when he was forty-seven, and priest when he was forty-eight; and when he was fifty he took his B.D. at Cambridge. But these things led to no advancement; they were followed only by trouble and difficulties. Two years after taking his degree Barnes lost his wife, and his six children their mother. Julia Barnes, a woman who had been beautiful, lively, sensible, and full of laughter, but never robust, died on 21st June 1852, and for the days after Barnes wrote nothing in his Italian diary but 'June 22, 23, 24, 26, 27—Giorni d'orrore'. Nearly a year later his diary says: 'Heavy-hearted for my as-tounding loss'; and until his death he finished his en-tries, night after night, with the word 'Giulia', written, as his biographer says, like a sigh at the end of each day.

For the rest, his life was, on the whole, even. When his school began to fail (excellent schoolmaster as he was), his friends procured him a Civil List pension of £70 a year; and ten months later, in 1862, he was pre-sented with the living of Winterborne Came, just out-side Dorchester. This meant an end of anxiety. It meant a comfortable and a peaceful old age in the rec-tory through another twenty-four years.

4

II

It was in these last years that Barnes became something of a celebrated poet outside his own county. Allingham had written to him in gratitude for his poems as early as 1850. Coventry Patmore had first cheered him with praise by 1859. Palgrave, Gosse and others came after. Yet in all his early life—and it would not be easy to decide how much of a handicap this really was —Barnes had had no friend or acquaintance, so far as we can tell, of his own stature. He knew, and was helped by older men with some scholarship and ability; but he was past middle age before he had any contact at all with another considerable poet. Most of his writing had been done.

He had not been aggressive; and beyond the approach to Ackermann, he never seems to have had a thought of moving nearer to London than Mere, or of introducing himself to any other writer. He liked Wiltshire. He liked Dorset still more. He liked scything, he liked his wife, his children, his pursuits. 'Mr. Barnes', his young wife would say to him, 'you are burying your talents in this poor out-of-the-way place.' And indeed he had a 'marked shyness of demeanour, an awkwardness in his gait and mien, and a certain indifference to his personal appearance'. He was 'morbidly modest'; and 'so uniformly mild were his manners and language that he was often suspected of being deficient in determination and spirit; a suspicion which in reality had no very solid justification; but Barnes was such a decided advocate of peace at any price that he would never, except when driven by sheer necessity, enter any arena as a probable disputant.' He kept good discipline in his school, never used the cane, and always wore (in the class-room) 'a long, light-blue, rough-faced, flannel-textured dressing-gown'.

That was Barnes in his twenties and thirties—an odd scholar and schoolmaster, bald-headed before his time, and content with the peaceful obscurity of Mere or Dorchester. The pupil—a relation by marriage—who recorded these recollections added that he was 'nearly isolated' socially, and was looked down upon in Mere, and in Dorchester as well. He had his few friends; but whether that 'nearly isolated' is an exaggeration or no, certainly all his richest years of creation were passed in a loneliness of spirit and intellect. Barnes, like his neighbours, was unaware of the comparative standing of his own genius, and the world was unaware of it until Coventry Patmore began to review him and praise him when he was nearly sixty. And then the world quickly returned to its old indifference. After his death, Tennyson, Browning, Arnold, Patmore and others signed a memorial praying the First Lord of the Treasury to continue Barnes's Civil List pension to the daughter who had nursed him. They state that in the last years of his life Barnes's income from his poems was 'about £7 only'.

Patmore wrote of him: 'He is of no school but that of nature', which is true, so long as you do not interpret it to mean that he was a naïve, or unlearned writer. 'Mr. Barnes, in his poems, is nothing but a poet. He does not there protest against anything in religion, politics, or the arrangements of society; nor has he the advantage of being able to demand the admiration of the sympathizing public on the score that he is a chimney-sweep, or a rat-catcher, and has never learned to read.' But for all his meticulous, highly professional knowledge of writing, and his rare gift of sustaining his sensibility and skill through life, I doubt if Barnes ever quite looked upon himself as a 'poet' in our conscious European way. He was fulfilled. He was much more like a plant, which does not exist for its flowers; and such a lack of vanity and ambition coupled with so much expert skill may be unique. If he had moved among men of letters, he might have gained much; but he might equally have stained the clear run of his talent. Landor might have companioned him well, and invigorated him, but who else? He was narrowed by Dorset; yet Dorset, for all its indifference, kept him safe, as Clare was kept safe in his asylum.

III

His first book was *Poetical Pieces*, printed for him in Dorchester in 1820—ten poems in ordinary English. He was then twenty years old, and there is nothing much to mark in these conventional album verses but their neatness, and the fact that he began to write in normal English, and for many years continued to do so. *Orra: A Lapland Tale*, Dorchester-printed in 1822, is worth more. It stands to his later writing like *Gebir* to the rest of Landor, or *Midnight* and *A Vision of the Mermaids* to the rest of Crabbe and Hopkins. The subject is Orra's search for her lover, a night she spends in a rugged cave, and the loss of her boat, so that the result (undescribed) must be Orra's death; and it comes partly out of his reading of Acerbi's *Travels through Sweden, Finland and Lapland to the North Cape*, a travel book published twenty years before, partly from that recurrent vision in eighteenth-century verse of a frozen sea. Barnes's unending love of clear, contrasting colour is now put down for the first time:

Her bosom seemed, beneath her long black hair,
    Like snowy hills beneath the clouds of night. . . .

As graceful as the silvery cloud
    That glides upon the summer air. . . .

And softly now her snowy eyelids close,
    Weighed down by slumber, o'er her bright blue
      eyes. . . .

There are three seedlings which develop in his later poetry. In *A Vision of the Mermaids* Hopkins's way of making a detailed jewellery out of his observation shows itself already lusciously and thickly. In Barnes's *Orra*, naïve as it is, you see already with how much care he is going to select; and how sparsely, and so how brightly, he is going to use colours for emotion.

Twenty-two years went by before Barnes brought out another book of poems—his *Poems of Rural Life in the Dorset Dialect* (1844)—though in between he wrote much on languages and antiquarianism and published several school books of a slender size. Yet first it will be as well, out of its order, to look into the *Poems partly of Rural Life, in National English*, which followed in 1846. It is a book almost as little known as *Orra*, in which the sonnets, and probably several of the other poems, were written earlier—the sonnets, or most of them, in 1830, when, swayed by Petrarch's spell, he was also writing sonnets in Italian. Barnes's poems never develop an emotional, or rather a psychological subtlety. Simple elemental feelings are made to pull upon our hearts by an intricate subtlety of rhythm and pattern. That subtlety he had not made perfect by 1830, so that the simplicity of statement stands out a bit too much. Yet I do not see why so classical and serene a poem as the sonnet on *Leaves* should stay obscured:

> ... Whether ye wave above the early flow'rs
>   In lively green; or whether, rustling sere,
> Ye fly on playful winds, around my feet,
>
> In dying autumn; lovely are your bow'rs,
>   Ye early-dying children of the year;
>   Holy the silence of your calm retreat.

And other poems to be remarked in this book are *A Winter Night*, *Rustic Childhood*, *The Lane*, and *Burncombe Hollow*. Two stanzas from *Rustic Childhood* will show Barnes's eye for light and for objects. Many nine-teenth-century poets observed exquisitely, but not many could order this observation so well as Barnes, and space it out with such an infallible effect:

> . . . Or in the grassy drove by ranks
> Of white-stemm'd ashes, or by banks
> Of narrow lanes, in-winding round
> The hedgy sides of shelving ground;
> Where low-shot light struck in to end
> Again at some cool-shaded bend,
> Where we might see through darkleav'd boughs
> The evening light on green hill-brows.
> > I knew you young, and love you now,
> > O shining grass, and shady bough.
>
> Or on the hillock where I lay
> At rest on some bright holyday;
> When short noon-shadows lay below
> The thorn in blossom white as snow;
> And warm air bent the glist'ning tops
> Of bushes in the lowland copse,
> Before the blue hills swelling high
> And far against the southern sky.
> > I knew you young, and love you now,
> > O shining grass, and shady bough.

The same qualities, not yet finally intensified and re-fined, you can read in 'The Lane', one of the poems Barnes had written on the alliterative principles of Old English poetry—again an anticipation by many years of Hopkins's concern with Old English. (Barnes had much else to import into the nineteenth century, out of the wide reaches of his scholarship and his curiosity.)

IV

Barnes's poems in normal English up to, and after

this 1846 volume, are more numerous and more accomplished than is realized, but in the Dorset dialect, in the three dialect books of 1844 and 1858 (*Hwomely Rhymes*) and 1863 (*Poems in the Dorset Dialect, Third Collection*) he certainly did come to the top of his classical perfection. Thomas Hardy had quoted from Barnes's statement that he wrote in dialect because he could not help it: 'To write in what some may seem a fast out-wearing speech form, may seem as idle as writing one's name in the snow of a spring day. I cannot help it. It is my mother tongue, and is to my mind the only true speech of the life that I draw.' That always struck me as rather a puzzling statement. It is true that having spoken in dialect as a child, for some time he probably kept a Dorset accent (as Coleridge kept something of a Devonshire accent). As a man, he could no doubt slip from English into Dorset English; but his first promptings were to write poems in plain English, which he did until he was thirty-four, and continued to do, at intervals, all through his life. It was in plain English that he wrote a poem to Julia Barnes after her death in 1852; and after 1867, for his last nineteen years, he reverted to English and wrote, we are told, only one poem in dialect. In other words he could perfectly well help it, and often did. Had Barnes made a statement which was obviously untrue? In his fragment of his own life he wrote a little differently: 'As to my Dorset Poems and others, I wrote them so to say, as if I could not well help it, the writing of them was not work but like the playing of music, the refreshment of the mind from care or irksomeness.'

And others—that is to say, it was a general statement about all his poems, and perhaps a deliberate qualifying of his earlier statement that he could not help it—as if he felt that if nearly true, it was not quite true enough.

Writing in dialect began as a preference, a choice

which Barnes made out of his philological delvings. His daughter Lucy confirms so much in her *Life* of William Barnes, and says 'when he began, it was as much the spirit of the philologist as the poet which moved him'. She quotes his statement that 'the Dorset dialect is a broad and bold shape of the English language, as the Doric was of the Greek. It is rich in humour, strong in raillery and hyperbole; and altogether as fit a vehicle of rustic feeling and thought, as the Doric is found in the *Idyllia* of Theocritus'; and in the *Gentleman's Magazine* in 1840, several years after his first Dorset poems were written, but several years before the first book of them came out, he affirmed that the Dorset dialect was 'purer and more regular than that which has been adopted as the national speech'. So, far from being a spontaneous act, this choice of dialect was a learned perversity, which he was able to carry through, since dialect had been his first speech, without the defects of being perverse. Once he began, he found he could do it by nature. Then, no doubt, he could not help continuing.

What I mean will be clarified by thinking of Doughty, who also set out to revitalize English, but by reviving, with an early dictionary always alongside his writing hand, the dead, unspoken language of the sixteenth century. Doughty is unreadable, Barnes is a delight. Barnes is genuine, Doughty a monster, and perverse with all the defects of perversity.

Gerard Hopkins recognized the truth about both of these poets. Doughty (whom Bridges admired) Hopkins dismissed. Barnes (whom Bridges despised, partly for his celebration of 'the supposed emotion of peasants') Hopkins had already appreciated for a good many years when Coventry Patmore sent him the three dialect volumes in 1885. He had some sharp words with Bridges: 'I hold your contemptuous opinion an unhappy mistake: he is a perfect artist and of a most spontaneous inspiration; it is as if Dorset life and Dorset landscape had taken flesh and tongue in the man'; and writing earlier to Bridges, he makes a comparison, the rightness of which I will not argue about, between Barnes and Robert Burns. Burns, he says, does not translate: take away the Scotchness and something ordinary remains, but Barnes does translate, and without a great loss. That at least is true. Indeed, a lack of knowledge of the euphony of Dorset dialect does not, to my ear, make it impossible to enjoy Barnes's poems clearly and intensely. There are two lines I keep among the furniture of memory, and keep in this form:

> The cuckoo over white-waved seas
> Do come to sing in thy green trees.

Barnes wrote:

> The gookoo over white-weäv'd seas
> Do come to zing in thy green trees.

The translation I make, more or less without meaning to, is much nearer Barnes's writing than, shall I say, Barnes's, or anyone else's reading of the Idyls of Theocritus was ever near to the original sound of Theocritus; and though I have no suspicion that Barnes ever wrote any of his Dorset poems first in ordinary English—in the English he habitually used in his reading, in his letters, and, I suppose, in his thoughts—the English versions that he did make of some of the Dorset poems are lively and authentic. The English version of *The Mother's Dream*, for instance, is not less good than the Dorset original.

V

There is a remark in Llewellyn Powys's letters that Barnes never writes about the sea. That is nearly, if not quite, true. He had no taste for the sea, one of many facts which mark him off from other poets and painters and writers of his time—Darley, Tennyson, Swinburne, Patmore, Courbet, Melville, Emily Brontē, for example. And there is a deeper explanation for it than a land-locked childhood, and Barnes's intense cultivation of his inland, rural imagery. He had no use for the swell and turbulence and endless width of the sea—for its lack of form. He is not a poet for expansive mystery, for crossing the bar, for the infinite in any way. Tennyson has to cross the bar. Tennyson in death has to put out to sea. That was typical of the anxieties of the nineteenth century, whereas the attitude of the eighteenth century had been to sail calmly along to death or to put in from life's sea into death's harbour. So Matthew Green wrote that he made

> ... (may heav'n propitious send
> Such wind and weather to the end)
> Neither becalm'd, nor over-blown,
> Life's voyage to the world unknown.

And so might Barnes have written. Barnes, on the whole, does not feel lost, or overwhelmed, or bound to fight against a universal ocean. He accepts, and does not interrogate, the universe. His form matches that feeling. However narrow Barnes may have been, the form and its variation in his verse is one of its qualities by which we may profit. He was not a fragmentary poet, or a Samuel Palmer with eight or nine years of lyrical vision and explosion. *White an' Blue* and other lyrics with such airy vitality and youthfulness were written when Barnes was nearly seventy years old. And often it is not easy, so much are his poems conceived or carried out as a unit, to isolate a stanza, a line, or a phrase for admiration. Coventry Patmore well remarked that 'often there is not a single line worth remembering in what is, nevertheless, upon the whole a very memorable poem'. The poems are rhythmically

united with the most delicate skill, and then tied together still more tightly by refrains which, while they
may be identical, yet sometimes advance the sense
stanza by stanza, as in *My Love's Guardian Angel*,
where the refrain is worked up to the wonderful emotional weight of its last use.

Judging from the one volume in the Museum at
Dorchester, Barnes in his Italian journal seldom put
down any more detail about the poems he was engaged
on than a laconic 'scrivendo versi' or 'versi scritti'. It
would not be easy to date their exact evolution or to
follow in date and in detail all his complicated experi-
ments in form, which he worked out mainly in the
dialect. Yet through all his books, from *Orra* to the
Poems of Rural Life in Common English of 1868 and the
small *Selection from Unpublished Poems* produced by
Winterborne Monkton School in 1870, with what remarkable persistence does he keep up his sheer skill!
Hardy noticed that 'on some occasions he would allow
art to overpower spontaneity, and to cripple inspiration'; but he allows that rarely enough, and his art is so
fine and certain that he seldom seems monotonous
through mannered repetition, or overworking, of successful effects. If I read Clare's poems, so deficient was
Clare in this cultivated strength of Barnes, I find my-
self overfed with the visionary substance of poetry,
which has simply been put down in the readiest, easiest
and most obvious jog-trot form. Barnes was less completely *in* the world of nature than Clare. He does not
achieve Clare's absolute hits—he is not a seer—but he
does not come down to Clare's dribble of absolute
misses.

Form to him was fitness: he wrote several things
about it, and he explored as well the origin and simplest
nature of poetry. 'Matters most interesting to me are
those belonging to man, in his life of body, mind and

INTRODUCTION

soul, so in his speech, manners, laws and works.'¹ As
for man, 'the natural man is unfallen man, as he was
finished by the hand of God, when He saw all that He
had made to be very good'.² And whatever fallen man
may be, 'the beautiful in nature is the unmarred result
of God's first creative or forming will ... the beautiful
in art is the result of an unmistaken working in man in
accordance with the beautiful in nature'.³ He maintained 'there is no high aim but the beautiful. Follow
nature: work to her truth'.⁴ But 'the beautiful is also
the good by reason of a fitness of harmony which it
possesses'.⁵ He admired 'the beauty and truth of colour and action in the Dutch school; and'—since he is
anything but Dutch—'the harmony, tone, and effect of
colour, even with bad drawing, and, in some cases, it
may be with a want of depth, in a work of Turner'.⁶ In
all the beautiful things of a landscape, he discovered
fitness—'fitness of water to irrigate growth, and to run
for all lips to the sea; fitness of land to take and send
onward the stream; fitness of strength to weight, as of
the stem to the head of a tree; fitness of elasticity to
force, as that of the poplar, and the bough whose very
name is bending, and the bulrush and grass to the
wind; fitness of protection to life, as in the armed holly
and thorn, and the bush, or ditch-guarded epilobium;
and a harmony of the whole with the good of man.'⁷

Harmony was a favourite word, and harmonic proportion a favourite topic, with Barnes. He wanted harmonic proportion in churches—'that too little understood and wonderfully neglected principle of harmony
in form as well as in sound'⁸ ought to be applied, so he

¹ Transcript of MS. 'Notes on the Life of William Barnes' by
himself, in possession of the Barnes family.
² Review: 'Patmore's Poems', in *Fraser's Magazine*, July
1863, p. 130.
³ 'Thoughts on Beauty and Art', *Macmillan's Magazine*, vol.
IV, May–Oct. 1861, p. 126.
⁴ Ibid., p. 126. ⁵ Ibid., p. 128. ⁶ Ibid., p. 137. ⁷ Ibid., p. 133.
⁸ Letter on harmonic proportion as applied to churches in
Gentleman's Magazine, December 1843.

15

maintained, to the relative heights of the tower, the
nave and the chancel. He framed his pictures and
bound his books in harmonic proportion. He held that
poetry must keep in with the fitness of nature and must
conform to the nature of speech and the natural cause
of poetry among men. 'Speech was shapen of the
breath-sound of speakers, for the ear of hearers, and
not from speech-tokens (letters) in books';[1] and dis-
covering what he could about the origins of poetry
from books of travel and philology and his own study
of European and Oriental literature, he believed that
poetry did not spring from cultivation or refinement,
but from elemental necessity: 'there has never been a
full-shaped tongue that has sounded from the lips of
generations of any tribe without the voice of song; and
... to a bookless and unwriting people verse is rather a
need than a joy.'[2] It is curious to find him down in his
Dorset isolation writing that 'the measures of song ...
may themselves be measured, not only by the steps of
the dramatic dance, but by the steps of a march, or by
the strokes of oars, as in the Tonga songs of the kind
called Towàlo or paddle songs, which Mariner says are
never accompanied with instrumental music, but which
are short songs sung in canoes while paddling, the
strokes of the paddles being coincident with the cad-
ence of the tune'.[3]

In English poetry, his own practice was based on the
Enlightenment; and no doubt he owed that salutary
basis, in part, to being out of the swim, to being
brought up in a countryside where the eighteenth century was still alive in the nineteenth; and to associating
early with old-fashioned men for whom the Augustans
were more important, still, than Wordsworth, or

From the 'Foresay' in *An Outline of English Speech-Craft*,
1878.
[2] 'The Old Bardic Poetry', *Macmillan's Magazine*, vol. XVI,
1867, p. 306.
[3] 'On the Credibility of Old Song, History and Tradition',
Fraser's Magazine, September 1863.

16

Keats, or Shelley. Such is the viable advantage of not always being modern, or up to date. He was little touched with an Elizabethan or a Miltonic romanticism, much as he studied the structure and prosody of Milton and the Elizabethans. Spontaneity, singing because you must, 'like the playing of music, the refreshment of the mind from care or irksomeness'—yes. But he read Dryden and Pope, and he quoted Mrs. Cooper on Waller's poetry, that Waller 'rode the Pegasus of wit with the curb of good manners'.[1] It would be interesting to know when he first read and absorbed the Earl of Mulgrave's *Essay Upon Poetry*, with its emphatic praise of Homer and its emphasis on 'exact *Propriety* of Words and Thought' in the writing of songs:

> *Expression* easie, and the *Fancy* high,
> Yet *that* not seem to *creep*, nor *this* to *fly*;
> No Words transpir'd, but in such *order* all,
> As, tho' by Care, may seem by Chance to *fall*.

Mulgrave, said Barnes, 'writes to fancy or genius

> . . . I am fain
> To check thy course, and use the needful rein.'

'Without *judgement*, fancy is but mad', he quoted, and he went on, 'A Welsh bardic canon says: the three qualifications of poetry are endowment of *genius*, *judgement* from experience, and *happiness of mind*.'[2] Paraphrasing Mulgrave, he liked lines which are written 'with a skill that conceals skill', that 'keep all the strait rules of verse, yet flow as freely as if they were wholly untied'. Then, 'we cannot but feel that kind of pleasure which is afforded by the easy doing of a high feat, besides that which is afforded by good writing'.[2]

---

[1] 'Plagiarism and Coincidence', *Macmillan's Magazine*, vol. XV, November 1886, p. 77.
[2] Ibid., p. 77.
[3] 'The Old Bardic Poetry', *Macmillan's Magazine*, vol. XVI, 1867, p. 307.

After all that, neither the complexity of his lyric dodges and formalities, nor his care (how different from much in Tennyson) to pick over his observation and select from it, and never or seldom to overcrowd, continue to be surprising, however rare they are in other men's poetry between 1830 and 1870.

To analyse Barnes's skill exactly, one would need some degree of his own knowledge of Italian, of Persian (Petrarch and Sa'di were his favourites) and of Welsh, and other languages as well. On his eighteenth-century basis of 'exact propriety of word and thought' he heightened his verse in every way he could, by setting himself tasks of every kind. There are clues to this heightening, and to his mind, in the elaborate exemplification of rhyme in his *Philological Grammar* (1854), a book which he 'formed from a comparison of more than sixty languages'. He sympathizes with all rhyming tasks which can be alloyed into the structure of a poem. 'A poet may impose upon himself any task—as that he will introduce some forechosen word into every distich or line, or exclude it from his poem; or that every line shall end with a noun; or that his poem shall take a chosen form to the sight; or he may bind himself to work out any unusual fancy.' He mentions George Herbert's poems in the form of wings or an altar, reproves Addison for calling Milton's matching of words of the same root 'poor and trifling', as in

That brought into this world a world of woe
Which tempted our attempt.

'However poor and trifling this figure might have seemed to Addison, it is sometimes very striking, as shown in the spontaneous language of mental emotion', and he gives other examples of this root-matching, 'called by the Persians . . . derivation', from Virgil, Sophocles, Crabbe, Tennyson, Cowper, Coleridge, George Herbert, Shakespeare and other Elizabethans.

Other poets of his age had taken from Elizabethans only an attitude, or fairy nothings (compare much of Darley or Hood), or insubstantial horrors. Barnes looked at the way they wrote, their word-repetitions, their collocation of two words alike in sound, unlike in meaning, their acrostics, their elaborate alliterations, and so on, which are paralleled by the elaborations and conventions of the Persian medieval poetry he so much enjoyed. The Persian poets and the Elizabethan lyric writers (and, for that matter the English poets of the Enlightenment whom Barnes learned from first of all) concerned themselves more with virtuosity of language than with originality of ideas. Beside the Augustan uniformity of common sense and a commonly held stock of knowledge, one could place the statement of the Arab historian, Ibn Khaldún, that 'the Art of Discourse, whether in verse or prose, lies only in words, not in ideas . . . ideas are common to all, and are at the disposal of every understanding, to employ as it will, needing no art'.[1] That certainly was how Barnes thought of poetry, elaborate in art, simple in ideas, and straightforward in effect. And he transfers much of the elaboration he discusses to his own verse—for example, from Eastern poetry the 'kind of word rhyming, or word-matching' called *adorning*, 'in which every word of a line is answered by another of the same measure and rhyme in the other line of the distich':

> As trees be bright
> Wi' bees in flight.

The Persians, he says, use an ornamental punning or 'full-matching . . .' a full likeness in sound, of words which differ in meaning. He used it in *The Wold Wall*:

> Ah! well-a-dae! O wall adieu.

[1] Quoted by E. G. Browne: *A Literary History of Persia*, vol. II, 1906, p. 85.

19

He used the peculiar parallelism of Hebrew poetry—
the principle of 'Tell it not in Gath, publish it not in the
streets of Askalon'—in *Melhill Feast*, for example:

> The road she had come by then was soon
> The one of my paths that best I knew,
> By glittering gossamer and dew,
> *Evening by evening moon by moon*—

or in *Troubles of the Day*:

> As there, along the elmy hedge, I go
> By banksides white with parsley—parsley-bloom.

Welsh and Irish poetry were sources for him. For instance, in Irish poetry, 'there is a kind of under-rhyme
called *union*, which is the under-rhyming or rhyming of
the last word or breath-sound in one line, with one in
the middle of the following one'. Here it is in *Times o'
Year*:

> Here did swäy the eltrot *flow'rs*
> When the *hours* o' night wer vew,
> An' the zun, wi' eärly *beams*
> Brighten'd *streams*, an' dried the dew . . .

But his most pronounced Celtic borrowing is the *cynghanedd*, the Welsh repetition of consonantal sounds in
the two parts of a line, divided by a caesura, which is
better known in English through its use by Gerard
Hopkins. The familiar instance comes as a refrain in
the poem so celebrated through its musical setting, *My
Orcha'd in Linden Lea*, in which the apple tree

> Do leän down low in Linden Lea,

where the *cynghanedd* consonants are DLNDNL/NLNDNL;
but there are plenty more, such as 'In our abode in
Arby Wood', or 'An' love to roost, where they can live
at rest'.

20

Hopkins was made a bit uneasy about this particular borrowing. He found his rhythms 'charming and char-acteristic', as they are, certainly. But Barnes's use of *cynghanedd* he did not think successful. 'To tell the truth, I think I could do that better', and he added that it was 'an artificial thing and not much in his line'. I believe Hopkins was half true, and half-wrong in not realizing how much Barnes's line was at once con-scious and unconscious art—half-true, because al-though Barnes's most perfect poems are sometimes elaborate tasks, they are usually ones influenced by his borrowings from world prosody, but not embodying them pure and direct.

Barnes's soul was not lit by sulphur, he did not, like Melville, measure himself against fate or walk on the sea-bottom, 'left bare by faith's receding wave', or wrestle with God, or hang, as Hopkins hung, desper-ately, on the dreadful cliffs of the mind; he may, as Hopkins agreed with Bridges in saying, have 'lacked fire' (though that is not always so, in my judgment), but he *knew* and felt as much about the function in human life, the origins, nature, and adornment of lyri-cal poetry, and its form, as any poet who has written in English. To paraphrase a valuable remark of Auden's, he disciplined himself and proved the power of his creative impulses by accepting the limitations of form. He created a system of poetry for his own use.

VI

I have quoted Barnes's view of nature, though not completely: man has fallen, and nature as well is not unmarred, but 'the beautiful in nature'—that is 'the un-marred result of God's first creative or forming will' and 'the beautiful in art is the mistaken working of man' in accordance with this unmarred result, which is good also by its fitness or harmony. The fallen working

to the unfallen.[1] 'Look for pleasure', Barnes wrote, 'at the line of beauty, and other curves of charming grace in the wind-blown stems of grass, and bowing barley or wheat; in the water-shaken bulrush, in the leaves of plants, and in the petals of flowers; in the outlines of birds, and even their feathers and eggs; in the flowing lines of the greyhound, the horse and cat, and other animals; in the shell of the mollusc, and in the wings and markings of insects; in the swell of the downy cheek, the rounded chin, the flowing bendings of the pole and back, and the outswelling and inwinding lines from the head to the leg of woman stepping onward in the pride of youthful grace; and tell us whether nature does not show us graceful curves enough to win us from ugliness, even in a porringer.'[2] And 'fitness' made him an enemy of veneers and shams: 'does nature make you a handsome tree or flower near your town, and slight her work in the wold? or light up your water for a crowd-sought park, and not for the wanderers in the wilds? No. Nature and true art are faithful. . . . We have churches with a fine, high-wrought street end, and brick walls behind, out of man's sight (poor Pugin's eyesore!) as if the builders worked not for good, but for man; and so a low aim has wrought a low work of art. Of such a sham some writer speaks somewhat in the following strain—for I quote from memory:

> They built the front, upon my word,
>   As fine as any abbey:
> But thinking they might cheat the Lord,
>   They made the back part shabby.'[3]

Nature must therefore be sifted for the authentic, for the beautiful in nature; and the heavy grain of this

---

[1] 'Thoughts on Beauty and Art', *Macmillan's Magazine*, vol. IV, 1861, p. 126.
[2] Ibid., p. 128.
[3] Ibid., p. 136.

sifting, its force, is concentrated into Barnes's epithets
—'green-treed':

> As evenèn aïr, in green-treed spring,
> Do sheäke the new-sprung pa'sley bed—

or 'sweet-breath'd':

> An' sweet-breath'd childern's hangèn heads
> Be laid wi' kisses, on their beds—

or 'dim-roaded' night, or 'blue-hill'd' as an epithet for
the world, or 'sky-back'd', for the flight of clouds, and
many more—epithets which are impressed with the
force of experience. He told Palgrave that 'he had
taken Homer, and him only, as his model in aiming at
the one proper epithet in describing'. And this sifting
gives his epithets a serenity and wide truth that one
misses in the particular detail of much Preraphaelite
description, from Tennyson to the passionate observation of Hopkins. Read, or broadcast to an audience
who have not the texts in front of them and do not
know them, Dyer's eighteenth-century *Grongar Hill*
and Tennyson's over-embroidered *Progress of Spring*
(an early poem, it is true), and one poem is fuddling,
the other comes to the audience clear through the simplicity and sparingness of its effects. Barnes's poems
are, for effects, half-way between the two; but riding
his Pegasus on the rein, he would never go so far from
the wide truth as Tennyson peering unfamiliarly into
the inside of a horse-chestnut flower:

> a but less vivid hue
> Than of that islet in the chestnut-bloom
> Flamed in his cheek—

Barnes holds the rein at some such limit as 'where the
black-spotted bean-bloom is out' or 'thatch-brow'd
windows'.

He keeps in with this restraint in preferring the

quickly-taken truth of descriptions of states of light, states of air, and states of colour—sometimes all three in one. For instance, in *My Love's Guardian Angel*:

> As in the cool-aïr'd road I come by,
> —in the night . . .

or

> High over head the white-rimm'd clouds went on,
> Wi' woone a-comèn up, vor woone a-gone;
> An' feäir they floated in their sky-back'd flight,
> But still they never meäde a sound to me—

or

> I'm out when snow's a-lyèn white
> In keen-aïr'd vields that I do pass,
> An' moonbeams, vrom above, do smite
> On ice an' sleeper's window-glass—

or in three stanzas from *In the Spring*:

> . . . O grey-leafy pinks o' the geärden,
> Now bear her sweet blossoms;
> Now deck wi' a rwose bud, O briar,
> Her head in the Spring.

> O light-rollèn wind, blow me hither
> The vaïce ov her talkèn,
> O bring vrom her veet the light doust
> She do tread in the Spring.

> O zun, meäke the gil' cups all glitter
> In goold all around her,
> An' meäke o' the deäisys' white flowers
> A bed in the Spring . . .

But Barnes's use of colour is often, as I have said, the setting of one colour sharp against another one, a visual antithesis, like two halves of a line in Pope balanced against each other. Long after he had begun this, he began to look deliberately for its counterpart and

warrant in nature, making a list of 'the contacts of sun-
dry pairs of colours on natural bodies', such as white
and black in the bean blossom, or yellow and orange
in toadflax or the brimstone butterfly. 'Nature is very
sparing of showy contrasts of warm and cold colours.
Red and blue are very rare, and of yellow and blue the
cases are but few; and black and blue are found in lepi-
doptera more often than white and blue are seen in our
Flora and Fauna.'[1]

Blue and white, all the same, was the coupling he
most often repeated, though frequently he set yellow
against black:

> There near the wheatrick's yellow back,
>   That shone like gold before the sky,
> Some rooks with wings of glossy black
>   Came on down wheeling from on high
> And lightly pitched upon their feet
> Among the stubble of the wheat—

White sometimes against red, elder flowers against red
campion, or

> Oh! the cherry-tree blossom'd all white
>   And again with its cherries was red—

Or white against green as in the cuckoo lines or *Zummer Thoughts in Winter Time*:

> When white sleev'd mowers' whetted bleädes
> Rung sh'ill along the green-bough'd gleädes.

But blue and white began with *Orra* (and even before
that in a poem in his first book of 1820):

And softly now her snowy eyelids close,
    Weighed down by slumber, o'er her bright blue eyes,
As bound beneath the cold and wintry snows,
    The azure wave of ocean frozen lies—

---

[1] 'Thoughts on Beauty and Art', *Macmillan's Magazine*, vol.
IV, 1861, p. 132.

and they were observed together again and again, in his wife, in skies, in butterflies, in flowers against sky or reflected sky. Examples are in *White an' Blue*, where the colours are the substance of the poem, in *The Water Crowfoot*:

> Thy beds o' snow-white buds do gleam
> So feäir upon the sky-blue stream.

—in *Zummer Stream*:

> There by the path, in grass knee-high,
> Wer buttervlies in giddy flight,
> All white above the deäsies white,
> Or blue below the deep blue sky.

—in *Not Sing at Night*:

> Or where below the clear blue sky
> The snow white linen hung to dry.

And blue and white well express the mathematics, the clear, the serene, and the harmonious in Barnes's make. Blue and white are the serenity of nature—the nature, said Barnes, which 'is the best school of art', adding 'and of schools of art among men those are best that are nature's best interpreters'.[1]

VII

We have too much of a habit of reflecting our discontent with an author's political convictions, or his political indifference, or his inconsistency, back on to all of his work, as though the issues of the sadness of our time were immeasurably greater than ever before in human history. We forget that there are still for each of us what we must regard as constant transcending verities, that what appears to be 'reaction' may be much more vitalizing than the thirty-shilling suit of

[1] 'Thoughts on Beauty and Art', *Macmillan's Magazine*, vol. IV, 1861, p. 132.

modernity or *avantegarde*, or immediate politics, that
being a trimmer need not imply a lack of inward truth,
whether the trimmers are Dryden, or Turgenev, or a
good many living European authors who have had
touches of Munich about them. Barnes may, in a very
good sense, be a minor poet; but not in the sense that
his writing is a mess of words occasionally lit by a
sparkle of pure intuition. And I may have suggested,
wrongly, if you recall the quotation from Patmore, that
Barnes was indifferent to the times, or separated from
them entirely. As far as not being indifferent possesses
value, that was not so. The anxious bewilderment between faith and science scarcely reached him, and
scarcely ripples in his poetry. I can only recall one open
reference to it in his poem, *The Happy Days when I wer
Young*:

> Vrom where wer all this venom brought
> To kill our hope an' taïnt our thought?
> Clear brook! thy water coulden bring
> Sich venom vrom thy rocky spring—

—the venom being 'what's a-talk'd about By many
now—that to despise The laws o' God an' man is
wise'; and he affirmed in another poem

> My peace is rest, my faïth is hope
> An' freedom's my unbounded scope.

'That is a subject connected with politics, not with
poetry', he said to his son when he reminded him of a
request that he should write a Dorset recruiting poem.
'I have never written any of my poems but one with a
drift. I write pictures which I see in my mind'. The one
poem, the early Dorset Eclogue, *The Times*, with its
fable of the pig and the crow, he had written against
the Chartists. He felt that the Chartists would unsettle
the Dorset labourer without remedying his condition;
and, with his views of God, nature, man, harmony and

fitness, what did disturb him, deeply, was the unfitness
he saw in the social development of the nineteenth century, and in the consequent decay of freedom; the unfitness which caused him to write the curious amalgam
of wisdom and simplicity he called *Views of Labour and
Gold* (1859), in which, not unaffected no doubt by the
Christian Socialist writing of the fifties, Barnes was
concerned 'to show the possible effect of the increase of
great working-capitals and monopolies on the labourer's freedom or welfare'. Two extracts will give its
tenor:

'The kindness which is done by capital when it affords employment to people from whom, by a mono-
poly, it has taken their little business, is such as one
might to do to a cock by adorning his head with a
plume made of feathers pulled out of its own tail.'

'It is more healthy to rack one's mind in effectual
devices to win a skilful end, than to work as a machine
without a free aim or thought: and so, as a Hindoo
poet says, to be like a smith's bellows, breathing without life.'

But Barnes's social views, simply consistent with his
views of the world of life and art, are only a stroke in
the drawing of a full portrait of Barnes. They are less
important than the wavy, mazy, slow, river-like rhythm
of his poem *The Clote* (clote is the yellow water-lily):

O zummer clote, when the brook's a-slidèn
So slow an' smooth down his zedgy bed,
Upon thy brode leaves so siafe a-ridèn
The water's top wi' thy yoller head,
By black-rin'd allers,
An' weedy shallers,
Thee then dost float, goolden zummer clote.

—less important than the rhythm with which he pat-
terned his life and his impulses to describe and sing.

There are poems which are slightly embarrassing, in which Barnes tails—I hesitate to describe it so—into a provincialism of sentiment; but his tailings are more innocent and slighter than the monstrous wallowing falls into the same weakness—not confined to Dorset —of some of Barnes's greatest coevals. And even his weakest poems are strengthened by their pattern and dexterity. In the narrow sense, there are not art-and-society reasons for urging that Barnes should be read, urging that he should have the status given to him ungrudgingly by Patmore, Hopkins, and Thomas Hardy. He may—and I think he did—give to English writing more than has ever been suggested or allowed. Hardy he very much influenced, and Hardy's rhetoric and pattern were the first to strike the authentic note in Auden's life: 'He was both my Keats and my Carl Sandburg'—the note and the Contemporary Scene. And how much effect did he have on Gerard Hopkins, who read Barnes when he was an undergraduate, complimented him by critical admiration, and put some of his poems to music? Both Hopkins and Barnes were after a revitalized language for poetry. Were Barnes's poems—to name only a little thing—the seeds of Hopkins's own concern for Welsh and for Anglo-Saxon? Is it entirely a coincidence of period and a consequence of identical aims that 'or as a short-stand-night-watch quick foreflown' and 'which at early morn with blowing-green-blithe bloom' are not lines by Hopkins, but translations from Old Friesian[1] by Barnes? Or that both invented their own critical terms rather than take them ready-made and devitalized from philologists and prosody? Or was Barnes not the instigator of much which has come down through Hardy and through Hopkins as well?

Yet these questions are only, again, the more trivial baits to reading him—to reading one of the few nine-

[1] *Early England and the Saxon English* (1869).

teenth-century poets who 'conceived of art, like life, as being a self-discipline rather than a self-expression'. Barnes, if he were more read, could become one of the healthy, if lesser, antidotes to the Romantic disease. He is not a rustic aberration; but just as Barnes kept in Dorset during his life, so he has been kept in Dorset ever since. The point is to deliver him—to extract him from his rather snobbishly affixed integument of mud; to exhibit his mind's cool-aired quality.

GEOFFREY GRIGSON

A NOTE ON TEXT AND SELECTION

The text of the previously collected poems in dialect is that of the final edition of 1879, in which both the dialect and dialectical notation have been modified. Occasionally in the poems from the first collection of 1844 and from *Hwomely Rhymes* I have preferred the earliest version in whole or detail (though Barnes's ear did not often mislead him in his revisions).

All those poems are included which in my judgment are Barnes's happiest and most pleasurable. Added to these are a few, such as the *Julia* of 1820, the first poem by Barnes ever to be printed, which clarify his poetic origins, or explain his development. It seemed as well to reprint *Orra* for the first time, from the rare pamphlet in the Museum at Dorchester. The *Cambridge Bibliography of English Literature* doubted whether a copy was known.

For the poems and fragments uncollected till now I have put through the sieve more than a hundred pieces which belong to his old age, are mostly in common English, and were contributed mostly to the *Dorset County Chronicle*.

For help in preparing this selection I am grateful to Col. Barnes and the Rev. Canon Barnes, the poet's grandchildren, to the officials of the Museum at Dorchester, where Barnes's books and manuscripts are preserved, and to my friend Aneirin Talfan Davies, who identified for me the Welsh poems which Barnes translated.

WILLIAM BARNES ON POETRY

WRITING IN DIALECT

To write in what some may deem a fast out-wearing speech-form may seem as idle as the writing one's name in the snow of a spring day. I cannot help it. It is my mother tongue, and is to my mind the only true speech of the life that I draw.

> *From the preface: 'Poems of Rural Life in the Dorset Dialect, Third Collection',* 1862.

SPONTANEITY

As to my Dorset poems and others, I wrote them so to say, as if I could not well help it, the writing of them was not work but like the playing of music, the refreshment of the mind from care or irksomeness.

> *From his unpublished 'Notes on the Life of William Barnes.'*

THE RULES AND CONTROL OF VERSE

When . . . a man writes with a skill that conceals skill, and his lines while they keep all the strait rules of verse, yet flow as freely as if they were wholly untied . . . we cannot but feel that kind of pleasure which is afforded by the easy doing of a high feat, besides that which is afforded by good writing.

> *From 'The Old Bardic Poetry' in 'Macmillan's Magazine',* 1867.

Without *judgement*, fancy is but mad. A Welsh bardic canon says: the three qualifications of poetry are endowment of *genius, judgement* from experience, and *happiness of mind*.

From 'Plagiarism and Coincidence'
in 'Macmillan's Magazine', 1866.

The keeping of many of the straiter rules of verse with clipping and breath-sound rhyme have been considered, by some, to be learned triflings, idle prettiness, or childish tasks; though we think that, in early historical and didactic verse, they were most useful as memorial locks, and, as far as they were at the same time pretty, they were more worthy of use.

From 'On the Credibility of Old
Song-History and Tradition', in
'Fraser's Magazine', 1863.

Root-matching is not likely to hold its ground in corrupt languages, where the forming of words from its roots is no longer much if at all followed, and where words formed from its own roots are given up for borrowed ones.

Addison says of root-matching by Milton: 'A second fault in his language is, that he often affects a kind of jingle in his words, as in the following passages and many others:

> That brought into this *world* a *world* of woe,
> Which *tempted* our *attempt*.

I know there are figures for this kind of speech, that some of the greatest antients have been guilty of it, and that Aristotle himself has given it a place in his *Rhetoric* among the beauties of that art; but as it is in itself poor and trifling, it is, I think, at present universally exploded by all the masters of polite writing.'—*Addison's Critique on 'Paradise Lost'*.

However poor and trifling this figure might have seemed to Addison, it is sometimes very striking, as shown in the spontaneous language of mental emotion;

whilst some of the greatest antients who have been guilty of it, are the prophets and writers of the Bible.

From 'A Philological Grammar', 1854.

NATURE AND ART

... The beautiful in nature is the unmarred result of God's first creative or forming will ... the beautiful in art is the result of an unmistaken working of man in accordance with the beautiful in nature.

The beautiful is also the good by reason of a fitness or harmony which it possesses.

Nature is the best school of art, and of schools of art among men those are best that are nature's best interpreters.

Does nature make you a handsome tree or flower near your town, and slight her work in the wold? or light up your water for a crowd-sought park, and not for the wanderers in the wilds? No. Nature and true art are faithful.

There is no high aim but the beautiful. Follow nature : work to her truth.

From 'Thoughts on Beauty and Art',
in 'Macmillan's Magazine', 1861.

SCIENCE, RELIGION AND BELIEF

Matters most interesting to me are those belonging to man, in his life of body, mind, and soul, so in his speech, manners, laws and works.

From his unpublished 'Notes on
the Life of William Barnes'.

It seems to us that we should always keep asunder outward world-truth (natural philosophy), which is rightly the end of inductive reason; and inward soul-

35

truth (religion), which is the end of faith; and that if we set inductive reason to work in the dominion of faith, soul-truth, we may become unbelievers; and if we send out faith, in the place of reason, to seek world-truth, we may be superstitious.

Our writers may deem that from our wide field of particular truths, and our tracking of general ones by inductive reasoning, they have a greater right than their forefathers to generalize particular truths, and that their hanging of them on a general one may help their readers to knowledge.

But whenever a proposition, which is given for a constant truth is too hastily taken, and untrue, it may mislead a reader into untruth; and may so far vitiate a history that a great frequency of such ones would make men little willing to seek the particular truths with which they are mingled; while a history of pure and well-arranged single truths would be good for ever.

From 'The Pyrrhonism of Joseph Glanvill', in the 'Retrospective Review', February, 1853.

LANGUAGE

I am . . . a 'lingual conservative'; and it is therefore that I wish to see the English a purer, and more self-enriched tongue, instead of being a jargon made up of four or five others.

From 'A Letter on the Formation of the English Language', in the 'Gentleman's Magazine', June, 1833.

English has become a more mongrel speech by the needless inbringing of words from Latin, Greek, and French, instead of words which might have been found in its older form, or in the speech of landfolk over all England, or might have been formed from its own roots and stems, as wanting words have been formed in German and other purer tongues.

Thence English has become so much harder to learn, that, in its foreign-worded fullness, it is a speech only for the more learned, and foreign to unschooled men, so that the sermon and book are half lost to their minds: whereas in Tuscany and in the west of Ireland, or in Wales, the speech of the upper ranks is that of the cottage, and the well-worded book of the higher mind needs no list of hard words to open its meaning to the lower.

Some of the mongrel form of our English has arisen from the slighting of Saxon-English, and other Teutonic tongues at our universities and in our schools, where Latin and Greek have been, to barely Latin and Greek scholars, the only sources of wanted, or at least new, words. . . .

. . . the foreign words were not of great need, inasmuch as words for things that came newly under speech, might have been taken from the word-stores of our landfolk over the kingdom, or have been made from our roots and stems.

Luckily our tramways and railways were first made by working men who used for things under hand, English words of their own, as rail, railway, sleeper, ballast, tram, truck, trolly, shunt, and a siding; but, when the railway was taken into the hands of more learned men we had the *permanent* way for the full-settled way, and the *terminus* instead of the rail-end, or way-end, or out-ending.

The Latin and Greek mingled-speech of the pulpit is often one ground on which the poor leave their church, where the preaching is, as they call it, too high for them.

Mr. Boyd, in his *Common-Place Philosopher*, says:

'Many a clergyman, who would not think of giving orders to his manservant in terms which that person could not understand, is yet accustomed every Sunday to address a rustic congregation in discourses which would be just as intelligible to it if they were preached in Hebrew.'

What we want for the pulpit, as well as for the book, and the platform, for the people, is a pure, homely, strong Saxon-English of English stems, such as would be understood by common English minds and touch English hearts.

The wording of one of our collects, 'By reason of our frailty we cannot always stand upright', is as welcome to the poor as the finer one which was once uttered in a church, 'We cannot always maintain an erect position'.

In the *Recollections of Oxford*, by G. V. Coxe, M.A., late Esquire Bedel, at Oxford, 1868, we find, as a passage of an Oxford sermon, 'A system thus hypothetically elaborated is, after all, but an inexplicable concatenation of hyperbolical incongruity'.

We should not reach the English mind or heart the more readily by turning 'He scattered his foes' into 'He dissipated his inimical forces', nor by making 'I have no proud looks' into 'I exhibit no superciliousness'. Nor would an officer gain much by crying, 'Dextral rotation' for 'Right wheel'.

It may be thought that Latin-and-Greek-English is more refined and lofty than pure Saxon-English; but refinement and loftythoughtedness must be in the thoughts, and it is idle to put words for wit.

From 'Early England and
the Saxon English', 1869.

Speech was shapen of the breath-sounds of speakers, for the ear of hearers, and not from speech-tokens (letters) in books . . . and therefore I have shapen my teaching as that of a speech of breath-sounded words, and not of lettered ones.

Some of Barnes's 'speech-craft' coinings for corrupt words:

For Preface:	Fore-say
Abstract:	Unmatterly
Accelerate:	Quicken
Accusative:	End-case
Atmosphere:	Welkin-air
Depilatory:	Hairbane
Deteriorate:	Worsen
Perambulator:	Push-wainling
Posterity:	Afterkin
Telegram:	Wire-spell

From 'An Outline of English Speech-Craft', 1878.

COMMENTS AND APPRECIATIONS

COVENTRY PATMORE

Some of our readers may ask, How is it, then, that the world knows so little of this poet? The reply is, first, that his poems are written in a dialect which, while it is almost as different from ordinary English as that of Burns, is spoken by a much smaller section of the British population; so that the number of persons who can take up his books for the first time, and read them off with immediate satisfaction, is not large enough to constitute anything like a public capable of impressing its views upon the larger public beyond it. If Mr. Barnes had enjoyed the advantage, for example, of being a Scotchman, our present duty would have been done long ago by others, and 'Homeley Rhymes' would have been household words in every cottage in England. As it is, this remarkable poet has been condemned to many years of obscurity as the penalty of having written in a language to which an ordinary English reader cannot become well accustomed without something like half an hour's reading—a labour to which it is not to be expected that such a reader should submit, in the absence of compulsion from some critical authority.

In the second place, the most essential character of Mr. Barnes's poetry, though precisely that which renders his ultimate position, as a poet, most secure, is little calculated to win immediate admiration from any but the perfectly unsophisticated in taste and the perfectly cultivated. The improved condition of taste, in respect of poetry, is a very common belief and boast. It must be remembered, however, that, though time and disuse have made obvious the faults of our predecessors, our own corruptions of taste, if different in kind, may be quite as great in degree; that exploded exorbitancies and conventionalities of language may have been succeeded by other exorbitancies and conventionalities; and that, a hundred years hence, the shortcomings and aberrations of the school of Keats and of that of Pope may be equally striking to the mind of the then easily impartial reader. That, at all events, the popular taste in poetry is not better now than it was a hundred years ago is a fact on which the really cultivated and carefully judging few are probably agreed; and this fact, we repeat, is strongly against the immediate acceptance of a poet of whom it is singularly true that he is of no school but that of nature.

In the third place, Mr. Barnes, in his poems is nothing but a poet. He does not there protest against anything in religion, politics, or the arrangements of society; nor has he the advantage of being able to demand the admiration of the sympathizing public on the score that he is a chimney-sweep, or a rat-catcher, and has never learned to read.

In the often-revived discussion of the relative merits of 'objective' and 'subjective' poetry, both parties have been equally at fault; the half-truth held by each being indispensable to the constitution of the whole truth which they have missed. 'Objective' poetry, in the full sense intended by the one party, and as involving no transcendental or subjective element, is not poetry at all, as anyone with the slightest tincture of poetic feeling must admit. On the other hand, purely 'subjective' poetry is an equally impossible thing, though Wordsworth and Shelley have approached the impossibility, in some of their pieces, almost as nearly as various modern writers in the 'old-ballad' style have approximated to the opposite poetic negation. The divine spirit of love and light is, indeed, the subject of all poetry, rightly so called; but this spirit is not in itself capable of being contemplated by the human mind as a separate entity. It can only be manifested by being directed upon other and external things. 'Light', says this Spirit, speaking by a plenarily-inspired tongue, 'is that which maketh manifest.' Sensible events and objects, then, manifested in their divine relations by the divine light, and expressed in verse, are poetry; and, whenever the poet enables us to see common and otherwise 'commonplace' objects and events with a sense of uncommon reality and life, then we may be sure that this divine light is present.

That 'slight but perpetual novelty', which a great critical authority has declared to be the main characteristic of poetic language, and which is only to be obtained by the perpetual presence, in the poet's heart, of this all-renewing light is, however, also the character of the subjects which the true poet will generally choose; and, if we carefully analyse any very successful lyric or idyll which at first strikes us as being simply a glorification of the 'commonplace', we shall most often discover that it has some 'motif', as the French well express it, which has this double quality of novelty and slightness, although the events and ideas which are set in play by that 'motif' are of the most simple and ordinary kind.

In choice of subject, as well as in that of language, the rule above indicated is obeyed with rare felicity and uniformity by Mr. Barnes. All true poets obey it sometimes—that is to say, when the tide of poetical feeling runs high; but most poets, in the greater part of their writings, hide the absence of the feeling which inspires this delicate poetic novelty by 'striking ideas', 'magnificent images', or, at best, by imitations and repetitions of themselves in their few inspired moods. We warn the thorough-going admirers of the modern school that there is absolutely no finery in Mr. Barnes's poetry, and that often there is not a single line worth remembering in what is, nevertheless, upon the whole a very memorable poem.

By this time, we trust that many of our readers are satisfied that Mr. Barnes is not only one of the few living poets of England, but that, in one respect, he stands out, in a remarkable way, from other living English poets. Between all the other poets there are more or less intimate and visible relationships. They might have written poetry, but not the poetry they have written, had none of their contemporaries or predecessors existed. But, had Mr. Barnes been himself the first inventor of the art of writing in verse, he could scarcely have written verses less indebted to any other poet. This is the more strange inasmuch as Mr. Barnes is a scholar in many languages, and has, as we have understood, his enthusiastic preferences for particular poets. Seldom before has the precept 'look in thy heart and write' been followed with such integrity and simplicity; and seldom before have rural nature and humanity in its simpler aspects been expressed in verse with fidelity so charming. We breathe the morning air while we are reading. Each little poem is as good for the spirits as a ramble through an unexplored lane in the early spring. The faith we soon acquire in the writer's sincerity is such, that words and sentences, which would pass for nothing in another poet, please us. 'A wise sentence in the mouth of a fool is despised', but a commonplace in the verses of Mr. Barnes is respected, because we are sure that it was penned by him with no commonplace feeling.

Judged by the laws according to which the high-pressure poetry of the present day is, for the most part, written, many of Mr. Barnes's 'Homely Rhymes' would not rank very high; but, if that is good writing which does us good, this poet may compare with the best—and, after all has been said, we know of no better general test of the merit of prose or verse than that.

> *From 'William Barnes, the Dorsetshire Poet', in 'Macmillan's Magazine', June, 1862.*

His language has the continual slight novelty which Aristotle inculcates as proper to true poetic expression, and something much higher than the *curiosa felicitas*, which has been absurdly rendered 'curious felicity', but which means the 'careful luck' of him who tries many words and has the wit to know when memory, or the necessity of metre or rhyme, has supplied him unexpectedly with those which are perhaps even better than he knew how to desire. The words of Barnes are not the carefully made clothes but the body of his thoughts and feelings. Another still rarer praise of his work is that he never stops in it till he has said all that should be said, and never exceeds that measure by a syllable; and about this art there is not the slightest apparent consciousness either of its abundant fullness or its delicate reticence. He seems, in fact, never to have written except under the sense of a subject that makes its own form and of feelings which form their own words; that is to say, he is always classic both in form and substance.

> *From 'An English Classic, William Barnes', in the 'Fortnightly Review', November, 1886 (reprinted in Patmore's 'Religio Poetae', 1893).*

He has done a small thing well, while his contemporaries have mostly been engaged in doing big things
ill.

> *In a letter to Edmund Gosse,*
> *1886, printed in Champneys'*
> *'Memoirs and Correspondence*
> *of Coventry Patmore', 1900.*

I am the only poet of this generation, except Barnes,
who has steadily maintained a literary conscience.

> *In a letter to an un-*
> *named correspondent, ibid.*

TENNYSON

(*In October* 1863 *William Allingham drove Barnes over
in a fly to Farringford to stay the night with the Tenny-
sons. Among the company was Julia Cameron, the
photographer, who refused Tennyson's request to photo-
graph Barnes, because 'she objected to the top of his head',
which was indeed—see the frontispiece—peculiar.*)

Tennyson and Barnes at once on easy terms, having
simple poetic minds and mutual good-will. Talk of
'Ancient Britons, barrows, roads', etc. . . . Dinner:
stories of Ghosts and Dreams. To drawing-room as
usual, where Tennyson had his port. Barnes no wine.
Tennyson said, 'Modern fame is nothing: I'd rather
have an acre of land. I shall go down, down! I'm up
now. Action and reaction.' . . . Tennyson now took
Barnes and me to his top room. 'Darwinism, Man
from Ape, would that really make any difference?'
'Time is nothing (said T.): are we not all part of
Deity?' 'Pantheism', hinted Barnes, who was not at
ease in this sort of speculation. 'Well,' says Tennyson,
'I think I believe in Pantheism, of a sort.' Barnes to

bed, Tennyson and I up ladder to the roof and looked at Orion; then to my room, where more talk. He liked Barnes, he said, 'but he is not accustomed to strong views theologic.'

William Allingham's diary, quoted in Hallam Tennyson's 'Alfred Lord Tennyson', 1897.

GERARD MANLEY HOPKINS

(*Writing to Robert Bridges, 14th August, 1879*)

I was almost a great admirer of Barnes's Dorset (not Devon) poems. I agree with Gosse, not with you. A proof of their excellence is that you may translate them and they are nearly as good—I say nearly, because if the dialect plays any lawful part in the effect they ought to lose something in losing that. Now Burns loses prodigiously by translation. I have never however read them since my undergraduate days except the one quoted in Gosse's paper, the beauty of which you must allow. I think the use of dialect a sort of unfair play, giving, as you say, 'a peculiar but shortlived charm', setting off for instance a Scotch or Lancashire joke which in standard English comes to nothing. But its lawful charm and use I take to be this, that it sort of guarantees the spontaneousness of the thought and puts you in the position to appraise it on its merits as coming from nature and not books and education. It heightens one's admiration for a phrase just as in architecture it heightens one's admiration of a design to know that it is old work, not new: in itself the design is the same but taken together with the designer and his merit this circumstance makes a world of difference. Now the use of dialect to a man like Barnes is to tie him down to the things that he or another Dorset man has said or might say, which though it narrows his

field, heightens his effects. His poems used to charm
me also by their Westcountry 'instress', a most peculiar product of England, which I associate with airs like
Weeping Winifred, Polly Oliver, or Poor Mary Ann,
with Herrick and Herbert, with the Worcestershire,
Herefordshire, and Welsh landscape, and above all
with the smell of oxeyes and applelofts: this instress is
helped by particular rhythms and these Barnes em-
ploys; as, I remember in 'Linden Ore' and a thing with
a refrain like 'Alive in the Spring'.

> From 'The Letters of Gerard
> Manley Hopkins to Robert
> Bridges', ed. C. C. Abbott, 1935.

I hold your contemptuous opinion an unhappy mistake: he is a perfect artist and of a most spontaneous
inspiration; it is as if Dorset life and Dorset landscape
had taken flesh and tongue in the man. I feel the defect
or limitation or whatever we are to call it that offended
you: he lacks fire; but who is perfect all round? If one
defect is fatal, what writer could we read?

(1st September, 1885)

> From the same.

(*Writing to Coventry Patmore*, 6th October, 1886)
You are not to think I now begin to admire Barnes:
I always did so, but it was long since I had read him
(Bridges is quite wrong about him, and off his ortho-
doxy). I scarcely understand you about reflected light:
every true poet, I thought, must be original and originality a condition of poetic genius; so that each poet is
like a species in nature (*not* an *individuum genericum* or
specificum) and can never recur. That nothing shld. be
old or borrowed however cannot be, and that I am
sure you never meant.

Still I grant in Barnes an unusual independence and
originality, due partly to his circumstances. It is his

naturalness that strikes me most; he is like an embodiment or incarnation or man muse of the country, of Dorset, of rustic life and humanity. He comes, like Homer and all poets of native epic, provided with epithets, images, and so on which seem to have been tested and digested for a long while in their native air and circumstances and to have a *keeping* which nothing else could give; but in fact they are rather all of his own finding and first throwing off. This seems to me very high praise. It is true they are not far-fetched or exquisite (I mean for instance his mentions of rooks or of brooks) but they are straight from nature and quite fresh. His rhythms are charming and most characteristic: these too smack of the soil. However his employment of the Welsh cynghanedd or chime I do not look on as quite successful. To tell the truth, I think I could do that better, and it is an artificial thing and not much in his line. (I mean like *Paladore* and *Polly dear*, which is in my judgement more of a miss than a hit.) I have set tunes to two of them which appear to me very suitable to the words and as if drawn out of them.

> From 'Further Letters of
> Gerard Manley Hopkins',
> ed. C. C. Abbott, 1938.

F. T. PALGRAVE

Working for love of his art, and for love of his fellow country-folk, he has never tried to fall in with the literary current of the day. In a 'subjective age', as Goethe described it sixty years since, Barnes has been obstinate in his objectivity. He is indifferent to coloured diction, to sensuous metaphor, to allusions and ornaments added for decoration's sake. Politics, religion, ethics, are only implied. He avoids all display of personal feeling, all self-conscious confession, all inward conflict, and, keeping his eye always on his object, leaves the reader to be moved or not by its simple presentation. . . . If his plain, ancient, objective manner appeals less to the sympathy of contemporaries, it has in itself certain sure signs of duration.

On our long roll I find no poet who has more persistently and single-mindedly aimed at the true end of Poetry, high and durable pleasure; who has striven more earnestly in the interest of healthy happiness. To no one does the phrase 'holy simplicity', *sancta simplicitas*, apply more accurately. His song is as fresh and spontaneous as the bird's; as an old poet [Henry More] expresses it beautifully, it was to Barnes

> No pains, but pleasure, to do the dictates dear
> Of inward living nature,—what doth move
> The Nightingale to sing so sweet and clear,
> The Thrush, or Lark that, mounting high above,
> Chants her shrill notes to heedless ears of corn,
> Heavily hanging in the dewy morn.

From 'William Barnes and his Poems of Rural Life in the Dorset Dialect', in the 'National Review', February 1887,

He talked . . . of his own work saying he had taken Homer, and him only, as his model in aiming at the one proper epithet when describing.

From Palgrave's journal in 'Francis Turner Palgrave', by Gwenllian Palgrave, 1899.

THOMAS HARDY

Unlike Burns, Béranger, and other poets of the people, Mr. Barnes never assumed the high conventional style; and he entirely leaves alone ambition.

pride, despair, defiance, and other of the grander pas-
sions which move mankind great and small. His rustics
are, as a rule, happy people, and very seldom feel the
sting of the rest of modern mankind—the dispropor-
tion between the desire for serenity and the power of
obtaining it. One naturally thinks of Crabbe in this
connexion; but though they touch at points, Crabbe
goes much further than Barnes in questioning the jus-
tice of circumstance. Their pathos, after all, is the
attribute upon which the poems must depend for their
endurance; and the incidents which embody it are
those of everyday cottage life, tinged throughout with
that 'light that never was', which the emotional art of
the lyrist can project upon the commonest things.

> *From 'The Rev. William Barnes, B.D.',*
> *in the 'Athenaeum', 16th October*
> *1886 (reprinted in Lionel Johnson's*
> *'Art of Thomas Hardy', 1894)*

Primarily spontaneous, he was academic closely
after; and we find him warbling his native wood-notes
with a watchful eye on the predetermined score, a far
remove from the popular impression of him as the naïf
and rude bard who sings only because he must, and
who submits the uncouth lines of his page to us without knowing how they come there. Goethe never knew
better of his; nor Milton; nor, in their rhymes, Poe;
nor, in their whimsical alliterations here and there,
Langland and the versifiers of the fourteenth and fif-
teenth centuries.

In his aim at closeness of phrase to his vision he
strained at times the capacities of dialect, and went wil-
fully outside the dramatization of peasant talk. Such a
lover of the art of expression was this penman of a
dialect that had no literature, that on some occasions
he would allow art to overpower spontaneity and to
cripple inspiration; though, be it remembered, he never

tampered with the dialect itself. His ingenious internal rhymes, his subtle juxtaposition of kindred lippings and vowel-sounds, show a fastidiousness in word-selection that is surprising in verse which professes to represent the habitual modes of language among the western peasantry. We do not find in the dialect ballad-ists of the seventeenth century, or in Burns (with whom he has sometimes been measured), such careful finish, such verbal dexterities, such searchings for the most cunning syllables, such satisfaction with the best phrase. Had he not begun with dialect, and seen him-self recognized as an adept in it before he had quite found himself as a poet, who knows that he might not have brought upon his muse the disaster that has be-fallen so many earnest versifiers of recent time, have become a slave to the passion for form, and have wasted all his substance in whittling at its shape.

From such, however, he was saved by the conditions of his scene, characters, and vocabulary. It may have been, indeed, that he saw this tendency in himself, and retained the dialect as a corrective to the tendency. Whether or no, by a felicitous instinct he does at times break into sudden irregularities in the midst of his subtle rhythms and measures, as if feeling rebelled against further drill. Then his self-consciousness ends, and his naturalness is saved.

From Hardy's preface to the 'Select Poems of William Barnes', 1908.

52

BIBLIOGRAPHY

POEMS

Poetical Pieces (Dorchester, 1820).

Orra: A Lapland Tale (Dorchester, 1822).

Sabbath Days; Six Sacred Songs (1844).

Poems of Rural Life, in the Dorset Dialect (1844).

Poems, partly of Rural Life (*In National English*) (1846)

Hwomely Rhymes; A Second Collection of Poems in the Dorset Dialect (1859).

Poems of Rural Life, in the Dorset Dialect. Third Collection (1862).

Poems of Rural Life, in Common English (1868).

A Selection from Unpublished Poems by the Rev. William Barnes (Winterborne Monkton, 1870).

Poems in the Dorset Dialect by the late Rev. W. Barnes (Dorchester, 1906).

Poems of Rural Life, in the Dorset Dialect (Collected edition, 1879).

Select Poems. Edited by Thomas Hardy (1908).

A Selection of Poems of Rural Life, in the Dorset Dialect. Edited by W. M. Barnes (1909).

OTHER WORKS RELEVANT TO HIS VERSE

A Philological Grammar, grounded upon English, and formed from a comparison of more than Sixty Languages (1854).

Views of Labour and of Gold (1859).

The Song of Solomon, in the Dorset Dialect (1859).

A Grammar and Glossary of the Dorset Dialect (1864).

Early England and the Saxon English (1869).

An Outline of English Speechcraft (1878).

A Glossary of the Dorset Dialect (1886).

BIBLIOGRAPHY

SOME UNCOLLECTED ARTICLES

'Pyrrhonism of Joseph Glanvill', *Retrospective Review* (1853).

'Thoughts on Beauty and Art', *Macmillan's Magazine* (1861).

'On the Credibility of Old Song-History and Tradition', *Fraser's Magazine* (1863).

'Rariora of Old Poetry', *Macmillan's Magazine* (1863).

'Plagiarism and Coincidence; or, Thought-Thievery and Thought-Likeness', *Macmillan's Magazine* (1866).

'The Old Bardic Poetry', *Macmillan's Magazine* (1867).

BIOGRAPHY AND CRITICISM

Coventry Patmore. 'William Barnes, the Dorsetshire Poet', *Macmillan's Magazine* (1862).

'An English Classic, William Barnes', *Fortnightly Review*, 1886. Reprinted in *Religio Poetae*, 1893.

'William Barnes', *St. James's Gazette*, 9th October 1886.

'Life of William Barnes', *St. James's Gazette*, 19th December 1887.

Gerard Manley Hopkins. In *The Letters of Gerard Manley Hopkins to Robert Bridges*. Ed. C. C. Abbott, 1935, and *Further Letters of Gerard Manley Hopkins*. Ed. C. C. Abbott, 1938.

F. T. Palgrave. 'William Barnes and his Poems of Rural Life, in the Dorset Dialect', *National Review*, 1887.

Thomas Hardy. 'The Rev. William Barnes, B.D.', *Athenaeum*, 16th October 1886. Reprinted in Lionel Johnson's *Art of Thomas Hardy*, 1894.

Preface to the *Select Poems of William Barnes*, 1908.

BIBLIOGRAPHY

Lucy Baxter. 'The Life of William Barnes', 1887.

C. J. Wallis. 'Early Manhood of William Barnes the Dorset Poet', *Gentleman's Magazine*, 1888.

Vere L. Oliver. 'The Late Rev. William Barnes as Engraver'. (Dorchester, 1925.) Reprinted from the *Dorset Natural History and Antiquarian Field Club's Proceedings*.

V. de S. Pinto. 'William Barnes: An Appreciation', *Wessex*, 1930.

Sir Arthur Quiller-Couch. 'The Poet as Citizen', (1934).

c

Julia

When moonlight is spread on those meadows so
    green
Which the Frome's limpid current glides by,
To mark its calm progress, to gaze on the scene,
May delight the poetical eye.

To one who in some remote climate has pass'd
A long absence from all he loved here,
How sweet the first glance of the land, as at last
To his own native isle he draws near.

But by far more delightful and sweet 'tis to gaze
On thy bright azure eyes as they dart
From under those tremulous lids their bright rays
And glances for glances impart.

The smile of the Muse may the poet beguile,
Or the smile of gay Nature in spring;
To others Dame Fortune's precarious smile
Its many enjoyments may bring.

I would envy no poet with thy smile if blest,
Nor at Fortune's dire frown e'er repine,
For Muse's nor Fortune's smile ne'er yet possess'd
Aught to rival the sweetness of thine.

ORRA:
A LAPLAND TALE
1822

Orra: A Lapland Tale

INTRODUCTION

There are who scorn the Muse's soothing power,
   And deem the rhyming art an idle thing
To please the wealthy in a tedious hour,
   And will not deign to hear its vot'ries sing;—
   Though Pegasus, they say, be swift of wing,
'Tis but a woful waste of time to ride it,
   And that, to want it seldom fails to bring
Each vain and hapless bard that doth bestride it.

Weighed down by worldly cares, and fruitless sighs
   To scenes of pleasure, and a happier clime,
Borne by the Muse, at eve my spirit flies:
   Nor do I think that this can be a crime:
   I never trespass on the sacred time
Due to the worldly toil by which I live,
   Nor hope to gather from my humble rhyme
The meed which nought but honest toil can give.

There is a land whose solitary coast
   Looks out upon the frozen Arctic sea;
Though few the arts her simple sons can boast,
   Enough that they are virtuous and free:
Oh! thither let the weary spirit flee
   Whose only hope in solitude is placed,
Who would desert the busy world, and be
   The lonely resiant of some gloomy waste,
And there that soul its wished-for peace may taste.

For many a weary wretch is doomed to prove
   The anguish of an ever-aching breast,

And coveteth the *pinions of the dove*
   That he may *flee away and be at rest*;
But he, alas! who wanders forth in quest
Of lands unvisited by human woe,
   Shall wander over all the world unblest:
For perfect bliss no man on earth can know.

O land of darkness, and of wintry storms,
   Oft do I wish, although I know not why,
To see those hills that stretch their snowy forms
   Aloft beneath thy cold and sunless sky,
   While deadly chilliness is in the sigh
Of gentlest airs thy frigid winter knows;
   Nor wood nor stream relieves the weary eye
But all is shrouded in accumulating snows.

They boast not there of conquests they have made,
   Nor mourn the deeds their enemies have done;
The shining helmet, or the warrior's blade,
   Has never glittered in that pallid sun;
   They boast no trophies from the foeman won,
And none have yielded to his mightier hand:
   No riches covet they—and they have none,
To lure the spoilers from a foreign land.

There in the fleet Pulkha, along the plain
   They glide, exulting in the rein-deer's speed,
Nor dream of happier regions, where the rein
   Controuls the gallant and the mighty steed,
   Where flocks around the verdant mountains feed,
And yellow corn embrowns the fading year.
   Nor are they less content, than those who lead
A life of luxury and splendor here.

Warm glows their summer, while the sky displays
   The solar orb, but soon that summer flies;

64

The wintry air soon chills the short'ning days,
  And suddenly the blasted verdure dies;
  Then gathering clouds, and wintry storms arise,
And the pale sun withdraws his feeble light,
  No longer striving with the gloomy skies,
But leaves the land to winter and to night.

I sing the sorrow of a faithful pair,
  The hapless children of that chilly clime,
For youth and beauty are not wanting there;
  Nor is ingenuous passion deemed a crime,
  Although that sweet companion of our prime
To them occasioned many a bitter hour,
  And lovely ORRA, in an evil time,
First gave her simple bosom to its power.

Young ORRA was a Lapland maid, and fair,
  But doomed to wither by an early blight:
Her bosom seemed, beneath her long black hair,
  Like snowy hills beneath the clouds of night
  Alas! that ever misery should alight
On one so beautiful, on one so young!
  Alas! that all the woe I must recite,
Should, from ingenuous love, have ever sprung.

CANTO I

The heavens are again serene,
  The summer sun on high is glowing,
Again the woods and vales are green,
  And flowers bloom, and streams are flowing.
  But whither is young LAWO going,
That thus, beneath the noontide heat,
  We see him up the river rowing
His little bark so fleet.

Onward he looks, the waters roll,
  Still winding through the gloomy waste,
And many a cataract and shoal
  He yet shall meet to mock his haste:
But though his bark were even-paced
With thought, alas! his speed were vain:
  The pleasure that he flies to taste
His soul shall never feel again.

To-night young ORRA's father gives,
  In yonder vale, a gay repast;
For there the beauteous maiden lives,
  And thither LAWO goes so fast;
Now see how bends his flexile mast,
And how his bark strikes up the spray!
  Oh! heaven grant the breeze may last,
For he but ill can brook delay.

Yet no repast shall LAWO share,
  Far other hopes inflame his breast;
He seeks alone young ORRA there,
  Nor looks for pleasure from the rest.
  And though no welcome be expressed
So near her reverend father's ear,
  The maid has smiled on many a guest
By far less welcome, and less dear.

And now he sees the destined vale
  Before him wide and far expand,
And furls at last his drooping sail,
  And moors his bark upon the sand:
  Impatient from his weary hand,
The youth has flung the dripping oar,
  And gladly now has gained the land,
And trembling stands at ORRA's door.

At intervals his ORRA's name
  He hears, with many a tend'rer word;
He knocks, but no one to him came;
  Again he knocks, but no one stirr'd.
  But now young ORRA's voice is heard
Far sweeter than the sweetest lay
  That e'er the many-tongued bird
Chants in the woods on summer's day. (*a*)

She sings—but not as erst she sung;
  For, though it be a lively strain,
It falters on her trembling tongue,
  And speaks a soul oppressed with pain;
  But her distress would never gain
The pity of that noisy throng;
  And ORRA, scorning to complain,
Thus cloaks her woe in lively song.

ORRA'S SONG

I stood by the ocean at break of day!
  My deer in the pasture keeping;
And low on the greensward a youth there lay
  In the shade of a willow sleeping.

His beautiful limbs they were dripping with dew,
  On the thistle he rested his head;
But deep was his slumber, and little he knew,
  That I bent o'er his flowery bed.

Then smiling, the stranger arose from the ground,
  And he shewed me the glittering sea;
Far over those waters my shallop is bound,
  He said, wilt thou wander with me?

O no, I replied, though I knew thee most true
   Of lovers beneath the fair sun,
Believe me, young stranger, in vain wouldst thou sue
   My heart is not thus to be won.

Then he looked in my face, 'twas a piteous look,
   And my hand he began to wring;
I know, he rejoined, thy young soul could not brook
   The woes that from poverty spring.

The sun glows on high, and the weather is fair,
   I will fly to the desert e'er winter begins;
The ermine I'll take, and the fox from his lair,
   And my bark will be laden with choicest skins:

And my bed shall be made of the dusky fern,
   Where the thistle is waving its purple flower;
And no more to my dwelling will I return
   Till I gain for my ORRA a wedding dower.

But still, I replied, though I knew thee most true
   Of lovers beneath the fair sun,
Believe me, young stranger, in vain wouldst thou sue—
   For my heart is not thus to be won.

    Those notes had scarcely died away—
      The cadence yet was on her tongue—
    When thus responsive to her lay
      Young LAWO sung—

'And tell me then, ORRA, was that the day
   When last we met by the ocean side?
And was it that coldness which made thee say
   Thou ne'er would'st be any but LAWO's bride?'

Her name young ORRA trembling heard,
  And, blushing, turned her head aside;
Her sire, too, caught the fatal word,
  And saw the blush she strove to hide.
'That blush by which thy cheek is dyed,—
Thy voice so tremulous and broken,—
  Betray thy love,' the old man cried,
'Nor need I any other token.'

Then fast from ORRA's azure eyes
  Full many a bitter tear there fell,
And her breast—as to the watery skies
  The sea will rise—began to swell,
  For ORRA loved her sire full well,
And love she knew to him was due;
  But then she felt a nameless spell
That bound her to her lover too.

Her sire with kind paternal eye,
  Relenting, marked his daughter's woe,
And sighed, and almost wondered why
  He should have frowned upon her so.
Ah! who is he that does not know
How sweetly woman's tears beguile?
  Or if his anger made them flow,
Who could withhold the healing smile?

Thus did the tears of that loved maid
  Her father's anger soon subdue,
But, ere his feelings were betrayed,
  Young LAWO, ent'ring, met his view:
'Vain youth,'' said he, "and who are you?
  Come you to mar our evening cheer?
Or will you join these fav'rite few?
  Whence come you? and what would you here?'

69

Thus LAWO: 'pr'ythee, Sir, unbend
   Thy brow, nor harbour idle fear;
I come not here but as a friend,
   Though not to taste your evening cheer:
   I am a wand'ring mountaineer,
Nor do I fear to own the name; (b)
   I've left my roving tribe, and here
Am come my promised bride to claim.

'While the mild summer yet was young,
   When last we to the ocean strayed, (c)
Ere yet the summer birds had sung
   Their thrilling notes in the woodland shade,
   My wand'ring tribe awhile delayed
Their erring course by the ocean side,
   To feed their deer upon the glade,
And fish in the now unfrozen tide.

'Once as I watched the grazing herd,
   Where trees a gloomy shadow threw
Around; as blithesome as a bird,
   I whiled my time with the sweet harpu; (d)
   There first that maiden met my view,
Who at thy side in anguish weeps,
   And there that passion first I knew,
Which still my heart in thraldom keeps.

'As graceful as the silvery cloud
   That glides upon the summer air,
She moved, a monarch might be proud,
   The love of such a form to share;
   I marked her shape, her flowing hair,
And eyes of bright ethereal blue,
   And Oh! I thought, a form so fair
The liveliest fancy never drew.

'The lovely maiden went her way,
　　There passed few words between us then,
But on the next propitious day,
　　Again we met within the glen,
　　Again, again, and yet again
She smiling came to meet me there:
　　Oh bliss beyond the bliss of men,
To share the smile of one so fair!

'I need not tell how warm a flame
　　Her beauty kindled in my breast;
And why was ORRA much to blame
　　If she a mutual love confessed?
　　But see, this Cup will tell the rest, (e)
O'erflowing with the nuptial wine:
　　Receive it—and thou mak'st me blest,
Refuse it—misery is mine.'

Young LAWO watched the old man's eyes
　　And read his doom ere he began,
Quick from his cheek the colour flies,
　　And through his frame a tremor ran;
　　'Youth,' said the venerable man,
'I cannot take the proffered wine,—
　　Thy suit alas! is vain, nor can
The maid thou askest e're be thine.

'Though not in her esteem hast thou
　　A rival—yet thou hast in mine;
And here his tribe are sitting now,
　　Rejoicing o'er th' accepted wine;
　　Thick as the stars in heaven that shine,
Are the deer his native fields display,
　　And boats to glide through ocean brine,
And sledges for the snowy way.

71

'He hath—though these alone, 'tis true,
   Can never make us blest,' he said;
'But thou art of the wand'ring crew,
   And hast not where to lay thy head.
   Then can that tender maiden wed
To join thy rude and roving band,
   Perhaps to beg her daily bread,
A vagrant in her native land?'

The crisis of his doom is past:
   From his full heart he gave a sigh
As if his soul would breathe its last;
   And downward turned his tearful eye;
   Nor could he utter a reply,
But muttered forth a faint farewell,
   And quickly turned for e'er to fly
From ORRA and her native dell.

And he again has spread his sail
   And, like an eagle on the wind,
He glides along before the gale,
   And leaves his ORRA far behind:
   But still in his perturbèd mind
Her image dwells, though out of sight;
   Nor can the charms of womankind
Again afford his soul delight.

CANTO II

Devoid is he of real tenderness,
   Who, though the blessings of this world denied,—
   Would wish the maid he loves to be his bride,
To pine with him in mis'ry and distress;
   For she can never break the sacred tie
By which her fortune is with his entwined,
   Nor leave the scene of misery, to fly
To the loved home she first for him resigned.

Unhappy is the fond ingenuous heart,
   That, in adversity, admires the fair,
   Yet would not they his misery should share,
But loves too well, by far, to live apart:
Angelic forms he sees around him glide,
   Whose smiles, alas, he cannot hope to gain,
Like Tantalus who lingered in the tide
   Which he for e'er essayed to taste in vain.

'Till now, young LAWO never mourned his fate,
   Though scarce a worldly blessing did he share;
But now he saw his rude and vagrant state,
   The beauteous ORRA was not formed to bear
'Oh! then I ne'er will ask that hand again—
Nor never build my pleasure on her pain—
   'Farewell,' he said, 'farewell, my ORRA fair!'

His ORRA's name he murmured yet again:
   'Farewell,' he said, and trembled as he spake,
'I ne'er will lead thy spirit into pain—
   Oh no! my aching heart shall sooner break;
   And yet, heart-rending thought! must I forsake
A maid so heav'nly fair, a maid so true?
   Ah poverty! ah ORRA! yes, adieu!'

Now thrice around the heav'ns the moon has rolled,
   And yet he comes not to his promised bride,
'Oh, is his love,' she said, 'so early cold,
   Who erst such vows of love to ORRA sighed?
And does he leave his ORRA thus to weep?
   Or does—but heav'n forbid!—my lover sleep
Beneath the billows of the ocean tide?

'He oft has told me of a little Isle
   High from the ocean, rising in the west,
Where, in the transient summer, for a while,
   His vagrant family are wont to rest;

73

And there perhaps my love is ling'ring now,
Ling'ring alas! unmindful of his vow,
  Beneath the smile of lovelier maiden blest.'

The Sun—for summer now is nearly past—
  Rolls half extinguished in the northern deep,
And o'er the land a twilight shade is cast,
  And singing winds around the vallies sweep;
The gloomy pine that shades the lowly shed,
In sullen murmurs waves its lofty head,
  And lulls the peaceful Laplander to sleep.

'Tis night—but darkness scarcely night resembling:
  Upon the lofty hills the sun still sheds
His midnight beams, in yellow spangles trembling
  Upon the snows that crown their airy heads;
And ORRA now has trimmed her little bark,
And on the heaving waves of ocean dark,
  Her swelling sail to midnight winds she spreads.

And she is gone to seek her wand'ring love—
  Ah! my fair readers! be ye not inclined
The maiden's artless passion to reprove,
  Nor say I make my heroine too kind,
For ye have arts—and eke I ween ye use 'em—
To hide the warmer feelings of the bosom,
  And vex, with long suspense, a lover's mind.

But ORRA loves, nor would conceal the truth,
  Nor cruelly an unfelt coldness feign;
And she would share the fortune of that youth,
  As now she meets the dangers of the main;
Where still to cheer her dark and wat'ry way
She sings, as on she sails, this artless lay:
  Oh listen to the Lapland Maiden's strain:

ORRA'S SONG

Oh many a time when tempests rose
   I've looked upon the troubled wave;
And wept as I have thought on those
   Who in the ocean find their grave.

And now were LAWO at my side,
   I'd sail for e'er from isle to isle,
Without a star to be our guide,
   And meet the tempest with a smile.

But may the tempest yet be still,
   The sun be beaming in the sky,
And be my lover where he will,
   To him I'll fly, to him I'll fly.

That I might think of him—he bound
   This glitt'ring zone around my waist,
And, till my lover I have found,
   It ne'er again shall be displaced.

The breezes failed, and ORRA'S sail was furled,
   On the still sea the light unbroken lay,
Save when around her oar the waters curled,
   Or when her boat struck up the dancing spray;
The breezes failed, and ORRA'S weary hand
Must fail ere she can reach the distant land
   Where she a while for fav'ring winds may stay.

Huge, rising from the sea, not far away,—
   And crown'd with glitt'ring and eternal snows—
A rock is seen, that in the solar ray,
   Far o'er the waves a gloomy shadow throws;
Its lofty head, as if rebuked by heaven,
Into a thousand shapeless peaks was riven:
   Nor flow'r nor plant upon its surface grows.

Its northern side displays a rugged cave,
   And the wild waters in the tempest, break
O'er lesser fragments now above the wave,
   That to the cave an easy access make;
Here, rising from their weedy bed of green,
The sea-nymphs, though by mortals seldom seen,
   Their watery locks in midnight sun-shine shake.

Here to the rock, her boat young ORRA ties,
   And gains the cavern, with as light a tread
As e'er those sea-nymphs from the ocean rise:
   And there her weary form to rest is laid.
Did one so fair e'er grace a cell so rude!
Or linger in so wild a solitude!
   Or slumber on so comfortless a bed!

And softly now her snowy eyelids close,
   Weighed down by slumber, o'er her bright blue eyes,
As bound beneath the cold and wintry snows,
   The azure wave of ocean frozen lies:
Sleep on, sleep on, thou miserable fair,
Oh slumber on, nor wake again to share
   The woes that wait thee, when thou shalt arise.

Fresh blows the wind—and hissing on the main,
   Like snowy serpents, curls the glittering spray,
Wrapped in sweet sleep, the beauteous maid is lain,
   And smiles o'er her unconscious features play.
The heavens with gloomy clouds are overspread—
Her wandering soul, in dreams delusive led,
   In sunny fields with LAWO seems to stray.

Loud raves the wind, the sky with thunder rings,
   And all is dark, save where the light'ning flies
Through the white foam that angry ocean flings
   Indignant to the dark and cruel skies—

From its frail mooring ORRA's boat is torn,
And far away upon the waves is borne
  For ever and for ever from her eyes.

Waked by the wild tempestuous war around,
  The Lapland maiden started from her sleep,
And pale and trembling, rising from the ground,
  Looked out upon the wild and troubled deep.
There glides a gleam of light'ning through the dark;
And in its light she missed her little bark
  That erst was moorèd to the rocky steep.

She gave one shriek, while tremblingly she laid
  Upon her breaking heart, her hand so fair,
And pallid as the surf that round her played,
  She senseless fell with horror and despair,
Nor can she gain her boat if she could leap
Down from the rocky height into the deep:
  Oh! no! 'tis death to go, 'tis death to linger there.

NOTES

Note (*a*)

'*Far sweeter than the sweetest lay,*
  That e'er the many tongued bird
  Chants in the wood on summer's day.'

This bird is the *Motacilla Suecica* or Scandinavian Wagtail, which, according to Mr. Acerbi (who travelled through Lapland in 1798–99), surpasses all other birds found in that country, by the beauty of its plumage and the sweetness of its voice. The natives call it *Saddan Keillinen*, signifying the *Bird of a Hundred Tongues*, and (it) is expressive of the nature of its song, which continually varies, and is an imitation of the voices of almost all other birds.

Note (*b*)

'*I am a wandering mountaineer*
Nor do I fear to own the name.'

Mr. Acerbi describes the inhabitants of Lapland as consisting of two distinct classes, the Maritime Laplanders, and the Mountain Laplanders: the former have settled habitations on the sea coast, and the Mountain tribes, like the Tartars and Arabs, are continually wandering from place to place, but generally move toward the sea in summer for the convenience of fishing.

Note (*c*)

'*When last we to the ocean strayed.*'

This alludes to the Mountain Laplanders going towards the sea-coast in summer.

Note (*d*)

'*I whiled my time with the sweet harpu.*'

The harpu is the national instrument of the Finlanders.

Note (*e*)

'*But see, this cup will tell the rest.*'

'When a Laplander', says Acerbi, 'has an inclination to marry a young female of his nation, he communicates his wish to his own family, who then repair in a body to the dwelling of the parents of the girl. When they are come to the door of the hut in which she lives, the principal spokesman enters first, followed by the rest of the kindred. As soon as they are come in, the orator fills out a bumper of spirits, which he offers to the girl's father, who, if he accepts of it, shows thereby that he approves of the match about to be moved for.' As Lawo goes to Orra's residence unaccompanied by his kindred, he is represented as performing this ceremony himself.

78

FROM

POEMS OF RURAL LIFE
IN THE DORSET DIALECT
1844

'Vita rustica sine dubitatione proxima et quasi consanguinea sapientiae.'—*Columella*, I, 1.

The Woodlands

O spread ageän your leaves an' flow'rs,
    Lwonesome woodlands! zunny woodlands
Here underneath the dewy show'rs
    O' warm-aïr'd spring-time, zunny woodlands!
As when, in drong or open ground,
Wi' happy bwoyish heart I vound
The twitt'rèn birds a-buildèn round
    Your high-bough'd hedges, zunny woodlands!

You gie'd me life, you gie'd me jaÿ,
    Lwonesome woodlands! zunny woodlands
You gie'd me health, as in my plaÿ
    I rambled through ye, zunny woodlands!
You gie'd me freedom, vor to rove
In aïry meäd or sheädy grove;
You gie'd me smilèn Fannèy's love,
    The best ov all o't, zunny woodlands!

My vu'st shill skylark whiver'd high,
    Lwonesome woodlands! zunny woodlands!
To zing below your deep-blue sky
    An' white spring-clouds, O zunny woodlands!
An' boughs o' trees that woonce stood here,
Wer glossy green the happy year
That gie'd me woone I lov'd so dear,
    An' now ha' lost, O zunny woodlands!

O let me rove ageän unspied,
    Lwonesome woodlands! zunny woodlands!
Along your green-bough'd hedges' zide,
    As then I rambled, zunny woodlands!
An' where the missèn trees woonce stood,
Or tongues woonce rung among the wood,
My memory shall meäke em good,
    Though you've a-lost em, zunny woodlands!

Leädy-Day, an' Ridden House

Aye, back at Leädy-Day, you know,
I come vrom Gullybrook to Stowe;
At Leädy-Day I took my pack
O' rottletraps, an' turn'd my back
Upon the weather-beäten door,
That had a-screen'd, so long avore,
The mwost that theäse zide o' the greäve,
I'd live to have, or die to seäve!
My childern, an' my vier-pleäce,
Where Molly wi' her cheerful feäce,
When I'd a-trod my wat'ry road
Vrom night-bedarken'd vields abrode,
Wi' nimble hands, at evenèn, blest
Wi' vire an' vood my hard-won rest;
The while the little woones did clim',
So sleek-skinn'd, up from lim' to lim',
Till, strugglèn hard an' clingèn tight,
They reach'd at last my feäce's height.
All tryèn which could soonest hold
My mind wi' little teäles they twold.
An' riddèn house is such a caddle,
I shan't be over keen vor mwore ō't,
Not yet a while, you mid be sure ō't,—
I'd rather keep to woone wold staddle.

Well, zoo, avore the east begun
To redden wi' the comèn zun,
We left the beds our mossy thatch
Wer never mwore to overstratch,
An' borrow'd uncle's wold hoss *Dragon*,
To bring the slowly lumbrèn waggon,
An' when he come, we vell a-packèn
The bedsteads, wi' their rwopes an' zackèn;

An' then put up the wold eärm-chair,
An' cwoffer vull ov e'then-ware,
An' vier-dogs, an' copper kittle,
Wi' crocks an' saucepans, big an' little;
An' fryèn-pan, vor aggs to slide
In butter round his hissèn zide,
An' gridire's even bars, to bear
The drippèn steäke above the gleürc
O' brightly-glowèn coals. An' then,
All up o' top o' them ageän
The woaken bwoard, where we did eat
Our croust o' bread or bit o' meat,—
An' when the bwoard wer up, we tied
Upon the reäves, along the zide,
The woäken stools, his glossy meätes,
Bwoth when he's beäre, or when the pleätes
Do clatter loud wi' knives, below
Our merry feäces in a row.
An' put between his lags, turn'd up'ard,
The zalt-box an' the corner cupb'ard.
An' then we laid the wold clock-ceäse,
All dumb, athirt upon his feäce,
Vor we'd a-left, I needen tell ye,
Noo works 'ithin his head or belly.
An' then we put upon the pack
The settle, flat upon his back;
An' after that, a-tied in pairs
In woone another, all the chairs,
An' bits o' lumber wo'th a ride,
An' at the very top a-tied,
The childern's little stools did lie,
Wi' lags a-turn'd toward the sky:
Zoo there we lwoaded up our scroff,
An' tied it vast, an' started off.
An',—as the waggon cooden car all
We had to teäke,—the butter-barrel
An' cheese-wring, wi' his twinèn screw,

83

An' all the païls an' veäts, an' blue
Wold milk leads, and a vew things mwore,
Wer all a-carr'd the day avore,
And when the mwost ov our wold stuff
Wer brought outside o' thik brown ruf,
I rambled roun' wi' narrow looks,
In fusty holes an' darksome nooks,
To gather all I still mid vind,
O' rags or sticks a-left behind.
An' there the unlatch'd doors did creak,
A-swung by winds, a-streamèn weak
Drough empty rooms, an' meäkèn sad
My heart, where me'th woonce meäde me glad.
Vor when a man do leäve the he'th
An' ruf where vu'st he drew his breath,
Or where he had his bwoyhood's fun,
An' things wer woonce a-zaid an' done
That took his mind, do touch his heart
A little bit, I'll answer vor't.
Zoo riddèn house is such a caddle,
That I would rather keep my staddle.

Woodcom' Feäst

Come, Fanny, come! put on thy white,
'Tis Woodcom' feäst, good now! to-night.
Come! think noo mwore, you silly maïd,
O' chickèn drown'd, or ducks a-straÿ'd;
Nor mwope to vind thy new frock's taïl
A-tore by hitchèn in a naïl;
Nor grieve an' hang thy head azide,
A-thinkèn o' thy lam' that died.
The flag's a-vleèn wide an' high,
An' ringèn bells do sheäke the sky;
The fifes do plaÿ, the horns do roar

An' boughs be up at ev'ry door:
They'll be a-dancèn soon,—the drum
'S a-rumblèn now. Come, Fanny, come!
Why father's gone, an' mother too.
They went up leäne an hour agoo;
An' at the green the young and wold
Do stan' so thick as sheep in vwold:
The men do laugh, the bwoys do shout,—
Come out you mwopèn wench, come out,
An' go wi' me, an' show at leäst
Bright eyes an' smiles at Woodcom' feäst.

Come, let's goo out, an' fling our heels
About in jigs an' vow'r-han' reels;
While äll the stiff-lagg'd wolder vo'k,
A-zittèn roun', do talk an' joke
An' smile to zee their own wold rigs
A-show'd by our wild geämes an' jigs.
Vor ever since the wold church speer
Vu'st prick'd the clouds, vrom year to year,
When grass in meäd did reach woone's knees,
An' blooth did kern in apple-trees,
Zome merry day 'v' a-broke to sheen
Above the dance at Woodcom' green,
An' all o' they that now do lie
So low all roun' the speer so high,
Woonce, vrom the biggest to the leäst,
Had merry hearts at Woodcom' feäst.

Zoo keep it up, an' gi'e it on
To other vo'k when we be gone.
Come out; vor when the zettèn zun
Do leäve in sheäde our harmless fun,
The moon wull rise up in the east
To gi'e us light at Woodcom' feäst.
Come, Fanny, come! put on thy white,
'Tis merry Woodcom' feäst to-night:

There's nothèn vor to mwope about,—
Come out, you leäzy jeäde, come out!
An' thou wult be, to woone at leäst,
The pirtiest maïd at Woodcom' feäst.

Evenèn in the Village

Now the light o' the west is a-turn'd to gloom,
  An' the men be at hwome vrom ground;
An' the bells be a-zendèn all down the Coombe
  From tower, their mwoansome sound.
     An' the wind is still,
     An' the house-dogs do bark,
An' the rooks be a-vled to the elems high an' dark,
  An' the water do roar at mill.

An' the flickerèn light drough the window-peäne
  Vrom the candle's dull fleäme do shoot,
An' young Jemmy the smith is a-gone down leäne,
  A-playèn his shrill-vaïced flute.
     An' the miller's man
     Do zit down at his ease
On the seat that is under the cluster o' trees,
  Wi' his pipe an' his cider can.

Maÿ

Come out o' door, 'tis Spring! 'tis Maÿ
The trees be green, the vields be gaÿ;
The weather's warm, the winter blast,
Wi' all his traïn o' clouds, is past;
The zun do rise while vo'k do sleep,
To teäke a higher daily zweep,
86

Wi' cloudless feäce a-flingèn down
His sparklèn light upon the groun'.

The aïr's a-streamèn soft,—come drow
The windor open; let it blow
In drough the house, where vire, an' door
A-shut, kept out the cwold avore.
Come, let the vew dull embers die,
An' come below the open sky;
An' wear your best, vor fear the groun'
In colours gaÿ mid sheäme your gown:
An' goo an' rig wi' me a mile
Or two up over geäte an' stile,
Drough zunny parrocks that do leäd,
Wi' crooked hedges, to the meäd,
Where elems high, in steätely ranks,
Do rise vrom yoller cowslip-banks,
An' birds do twitter vrom the spraÿ
O' bushes deck'd wi' snow-white maÿ;
An' gil'cups, wi' the deäisy bed,
Be under ev'ry step you tread.

We'll wind up roun' the hill, an' look
All down the thickly-timber'd nook,
Out where the squier's house do show
His grey-wall'd peaks up drough the row
O' sheädy elems, where the rook
Do build her nest; an' where the brook
Do creep along the meäds, an' lie
To catch the brightness o' the sky;
An' cows, in water to theïr knees,
Do stan' a-whiskèn off the vlees.

Mother o' blossoms, and ov all
That's feäir a-vield vrom Spring till Fall,
The gookoo over white-weäv'd seas
Do come to zing in thy green trees,

An' buttervlees, in giddy flight,
Do gleäm the mwost by thy gaÿ light.
Oh! when, at last, my fleshly eyes
Shall shut upon the vields an' skies,
Mid zummer's zunny days be gone,
An' winter's clouds be comèn on:
Nor mid I draw upon the e'th,
O' thy sweet aïr my leätest breath;
Alassen I mid want to staÿ
Behine' for thee, O flow'ry Maÿ!

The White Road up athirt the Hill

When hot-beam'd zuns do strik right down,
An' burn our zweaty feäzen brown;
An' zunny slopes, a-lyèn nigh,
Be back'd by hills so blue's the sky;
Then, while the bells do sweetly cheem
Upon the champèn high-neck'd team,
How lively, wi' a friend, do seem
   The white road up athirt the hill.

The zwellèn downs, wi' chalky tracks
A-climmèn up their zunny backs,
Do hide green meäds an' zedgy brooks,
An' clumps o' trees wi' glossy rooks,
An' hearty vo'k to laugh an' zing,
An' parish-churches in a string,
Wi' tow'rs o' merry bells to ring,
   An' white roads up athirt the hills.

At feäst, when uncle's vo'k do come
To spend the day wi' us at hwome,
An' we do lay upon the bwoard
The very best we can avvword,
The wolder woones do talk an' smoke,
An' younger woones do plaÿ an' joke,
88

An' in the evenèn all our vo'k
  Do bring em gwaïn athirt the hill.

An' while the green do zwarm wi' wold
An' young, so thick as sheep in vwold,
The bellows in the blacksmith's shop,
An' miller's moss-green wheel do stop,
An' lwonesome in the wheelwright's shed
'S a-left the wheelless waggon-bed;
While zwarms o' comèn friends do tread
  The white road down athirt the hill.

An' when the windèn road so white,
A-climmèn up the hills in zight,
Do leäd to pleäzen, east or west,
The vu'st a-known, an' lov'd the best,
How touchèn in the zunsheen's glow,
Or in the sheädes that clouds do drow
Upon the zunburnt downs below,
  'S the white road up athirt the hill.

What peaceful hollows here the long
White roads do windy round among!
Wi' deäiry cows in woody nooks,
An' haymeäkers among their pooks,
An' housen that the trees do screen
From zun an' zight by boughs o' green!
Young blushèn beauty's hwomes between
  The white roads up athirt the hills.

The Shepherd o' the Farm

Oh! I be Shepherd o' the farm,
  Wi' tinklèn bells an' sheep-dog's bark,
An' wi' my crook athirt my eärm,
  Here I do rove below the lark.

An' I do bide all day among
   The bleäten sheep, an' pitch their vwold;
An' when the evenèn sheädes be long,
   Do zee em all a-penn'd an' twold.

An' I do zee the friskèn lam's,
   Wi' swingèn taïls an' woolly lags,
A-playèn roun' their veedèn dams,
   An' pullèn o' their milky bags.

An' I bezide a hawthorn tree,
   Do' zit upon the zunny down,
While sheädes o' zummer clouds do vlee
   Wi' silent flight along the groun'.

An' there, among the many cries
   O' sheep an' lambs, my dog do pass
A zultry hour, wi' blinkèn eyes,
   An' nose a-stratch'd upon the grass;

But, in a twinklèn, at my word,
   He's all awake, an' up, an' gone
Out roun' the sheep lik' any bird,
   To do what he's a-zent upon.

An' I do goo to washèn pool,
   A-sousèn over head an' ears
The shaggy sheep, to cleän their wool
   An' meäke em ready vor the sheärs.

An' when the sheärèn time do come,
   Then we do work vrom dawn till dark;
Where zome do shear the sheep, and zome
   Do mark their zides wi' meäster's mark.

An' when the shearèn's all a-done,
   Then we do eat, an' drink, an' zing,

In meäster's kitchen till the tun
  Wi' merry sounds do sheäke an' ring.

Oh! I be Shepherd o' the farm,
  Wi' tinklèn bells an' sheep dog's bark.
An' wi' my crook athirt my eärm,
  Here I do rove below the lark.

Woodley

Sweet Woodley! oh! how fresh an' gaÿ
Thy leänes an' vields be now in Maÿ,
The while the broad-leav'd clotes do zwim
In brooks wi' gil-cups at the brim;
An' yoller cowslip-beds do grow
By thorns in blooth so white as snow;
An' win' do come vrom copse wi' smells
O' graegles wi' their hangèn bells!

Though time do dreve me on, my mind
Do turn in love to thee behind,
The seäme's a bulrush that's a-shook
By wind a-blowèn up the brook:
The curlèn stream would dreve en down,
But plaÿsome aïr do turn en roun',
An' meäke en seem to bend wi' love
To zunny hollows up above.

Thy tower still do overlook
The woody knaps an' windèn brook,
An' leäne's wi' here an' there a hatch,
An' house wi' elem-sheäded thatch,
An' vields where chaps do vur outdo
The Zunday sky, wi' cwoats o' blue;
An' maïdens' frocks do vur surpass
The whitest deäsies in the grass.

91

What peals to-day from thy wold tow'r
Do strike upon the zummer flow'r,
As all the club, wi' dousty lags,
Do walk wi' poles an' flappèn flags,
An' wind, to music, roun' between
A zwarm o' v'ok upon the green!
Though time do dreve me on, my mind
Do turn wi' love to thee behind.

Sleep did come wi' the Dew

O when our zun's a-zinkèn low,
How soft's the light his feäce do drow
Upon the backward road our mind
Do turn an' zee a-left behind;
When we, in childhood's days did vind
Our jaÿ among the gil'cup flow'rs,
All drough the zummer's zunny hours;
    An' sleep did come wi' the dew.

An' afterwards, when we did zweat
A tweilèn in the zummer het,
An' when our daily work wer done
Did meet to have our evenèn fun:
Till up above the zettèn zun
The sky wer blushèn in the west,
An' we laid down in peace to rest,
    An' sleep did come wi' the dew.

Ah! zome do turn—but tidden right—
The night to day, an' day to night;
But we do zee the vu'st red streak
O' mornèn, when the day do break;
Zoo we don't grow up peäle an' weak,
But we do work wi' health an' strength,
Vrom mornèn drough the whole day's length,
    An' sleep do come wi' the dew.

An' when, at last, our e'thly light
Is jist a-drawèn in to night,
We mid be sure that God above,
If we be true when he do prove
Our stedvast faïth an' thankvul love,
Wull do vor us what mid be best,
An' teäke us into endless rest,
    As sleep do come wi' the dew.

Rivers don't gi'e Out

The brook I left below the rank
Ov alders that do sheäde his bank,
A-runnèn down to dreve the mill
Below the knap, 's a runnèn still;
The creepèn days an' weeks do vill
    Up years, an' meäke wold things o' new,
    An' vok' do come, an' live, an' goo,
    But rivers don't gi'e out, John.

The leaves that in the spring do shoot
Zo green, in fall be under voot;
Maÿ flow'rs do grow vor June to burn,
An' milk-white blooth o' trees do kern,
An' ripen on, an' vall in turn;
    The miller's moss-green wheel mid rot,
    An' he mid die an' be vorgot,
    But rivers don't gi'e out, John.

A vew short years do bring an' rear
A maïd—as Jeäne wer—young an' feäir,
An' vewer zummer-ribbons, tied
In Zunday knots, do feäde bezide
Her cheäk avore her bloom ha' died:
    Her youth won't staÿ,—her rwosy look
    'S a feädèn flow'r, but time's a brook
    To run an' not gi'e out, John.

An' yet, while things do come an' goo,
God's love is steadvast, John, an' true;
If winter vrost do chill the ground,
　'Tis but to bring the zummer round,
All's well a-lost where He's a-vound,
　　Vor if 'tis right, vor Chrīstes seäke
　　He'll gi'e us mwore than he do teäke,—
　　　His goodness don't gi'e out, John.

Hay-meäken

'Tis merry ov a zummer's day,
Where vo'k be out a-meäkèn haÿ;
Where men an' women, in a string,
Do ted or turn the grass, an' zing,
Wi' cheemèn vaïces, merry zongs,
A-tossèn o' their sheenèn prongs
Wi' eärms a-zwangèn left an' right,
In colour'd gowns an' shirtsleeves white;
Or, wider spread, a reäkèn round
The rwosy hedges o' the ground,
Where Sam do zee the speckled sneäke,
An' try to kill en wi' his reäke;
An' Poll do jump about an' squall,
To zee the twistèn slooworm crawl.

'Tis merry where a gaÿ-tongued lot
Ov haÿ-meäkers be all a-squot,
On lightly-russlèn haÿ, a-spread
Below an elem's lofty head,
To rest their weary limbs an' munch
Their bit o' dinner, or their nunch;
Where teethy reäkes do lie all round
By picks a-stuck up into ground.
An' wi' their vittles in their laps,

An' in their hornen cups their draps
O' cider sweet, or frothy eäle,
Their tongues do run wi' joke an' teäle.
An' when the zun, so low an' red,
Do sheen above the leafy head
O' zome broad tree, a-rizèn high
Avore the vi'ry western sky,
'Tis merry where all han's do goo
Athirt the groun', by two an' two,
A-reäkèn, over humps an' hollors,
The russlèn grass up into rollers.
An' woone do row it into line,
An' woone do clwose it up behine;
An' after them the little bwoys
Do stride an' fling their eärms all woys,
Wi' busy picks, an' proud young looks
A-meäkèn up their tiny pooks.
An' zoo 'tis merry out among
The vo'k in haÿ-vield all day long.

Hay-carrèn

'Tis merry ov a zummer's day,
When vo'k be out a-halèn haÿ,
Where boughs, a-spread upon the ground,
Do meäke the staddle big an' round;
An' grass do stand in pook, or lie
In long-back'd weäles or parsels, dry.
There I do vind it stir my heart
To hear the frothèn hosses snort,
A-halèn on, wi' sleek-heäir'd hides,
The red-wheel'd waggon's deep-blue zides.
Aye; let me have woone cup o' drink,
An' hear the linky harness clink,
An' then my blood do run so warm,
An' put sich strangth 'ithin my eärm,

That I do long to toss a pick,
A-pitchèn or a-meäkèn rick.

The bwoy is at the hosse's head,
An' up upon the waggon bed
The lwoaders, strong o' eärm do stan',
At head, an' back at tail, a man,
Wi' skill to build the lwoad upright
An' bind the vwolded corners tight;
An' at each zide ō'm, sprack an' strong,
A pitcher wi' his long-stem'd prong,
Avore the best two women now
A-call'd to reäky after plough.

When I do pitchy, 'tis my pride
Vor Jenny Hine to reäke my zide,
An' zee her fling her reäke, an' reach
So vur, an' teäke in sich a streech;
An' I don't shatter haÿ, an' meäke
Mwore work than needs vor Jenny's reäke.
I'd sooner zee the weäles' high rows
Lik' hedges up above my nose,
Than have light work myzelf, an' vind
Poor Jeäne a-beät an' left behind;
Vor she would sooner drop down dead.
Than let the pitchers get a-head.

'Tis merry at the rick to zee
How picks do wag, an' haÿ do vlee.
While woone's unlwoadèn, woone do teäke
The pitches in; an' zome do meäke
The lofty rick upright an' roun',
An' tread en hard, an' reäke en down,
An' tip en, when the zun do zet,
To shoot a sudden vall o' wet.
An' zoo 'tis merry any day
Where vo'k be out a-carrèn haÿ.

Where we did keep our Flagon

When we in mornèn had a-drow'd
The grass or russlèn haÿ abrode,
The lit'some maïdens an' the chaps,
Wi' bits o' nunchèns in their laps,
Did all zit down upon the knaps
    Up there, in under hedge, below
    The highest elem o' the row,
       Where we did keep our flagon.

There we could zee green vields at hand,
Avore a hunderd on beyand,
An' rows o' trees in hedges roun'
Green meäds, an' zummerleäzes brown,
An' thorns upon the zunny down,
    While aïer, vrom the rockèn zedge
    In brook, did come along the hedge,
       Where we did keep our flagon.

There laughèn chaps did try in plaÿ
To bury maïdens up in haÿ,
As gigglèn maïdens tried to roll
The chaps down into zome deep hole,
Or sting wi' nettles woone o'm's poll;
    While John did hele out each his drap
    O' eäle or cider, in his lap
       Where he did keep the flagon.

Woone day there spun a whirlwind by
Where Jenny's clothes wer out to dry;
An' off vled frocks, a'most a-catch'd
By smock-frocks wi' their sleeves outstratch'd,
An' caps a-frill'd an' eäperns patch'd;
    An' she a-steärèn in a fright,
    Wer glad enough to zee em light
       Where we did keep our flagon.

An' when white clover wer a-sprung
Among the eegrass, green an' young,
An' elder-flowers wer a-spread
Among the rwosen white an' red,
An' honeyzucks wi' hangèn head,—
 O' Zunday evenèns we did zit
 To look all roun' the grounds a bit,
  Where we'd a-kept our flagon.

The Sky a-Clearèn

The drevèn scud that overcast
The zummer sky is all a-past,
An' softer aïr, a-blowèn drough
The quiv'rèn boughs, do sheäke the vew
Last raïn drops off the leaves lik' dew;
 An' peäviers, now a-gettèn dry,
 Do steam below the zunny sky
  That's now so vast a-cleärèn.

The sheädes that wer a-lost below
The stormy cloud, ageän do show
Their mockèn sheäpes below the light;
An' house-walls be a-lookèn white,
An' vo'k do stir woonce mwore in zight,
 An' busy birds upon the wing
 Do whiver roun' the boughs an' zing,
  To zee the sky a-clearèn.

Below the hill's an ash; below
The ash, white elder-flow'rs do blow;
Below the elder is a bed
O' robinhoods o' blushèn red;
An' there, wi' nunches all a-spread,
 The haÿ-meäkers, wi' each a cup
 O' drink, do smile to zee hold up
  The raïn, an' sky a-cleärèn.

'Mid blushèn maïdens, wi' their zong,
Still draw their white-stemm'd reäkes among
The long-back'd weäles an' new-meäde pooks,
By brown-stemm'd trees an' cloty brooks;
But have noo call to spweil their looks
    By work, that God could never meäke
    Their weaker han's to underteäke,
       Though skies mid be a-cleärèn.

'Tis wrong vor women's han's to clips
The zull an' reap-hook, speädes an' whips;
An' men abroad, should leäve, by right,
Woone faïthful heart at hwome to light
Their bit o' vier up at night,
    An' hang upon the hedge to dry
    Their snow-white linen, when the sky
       In winter is a-cleärèn.

The Evenèn Star o' Zummer

When vu'st along theäse road vrom mill,
I zeed ye hwome all up the hill,
The poplar tree, so straïght an' tall,
Did rustle by the watervall;
An' in the leäze the cows wer all
    A-lyèn down to teäke their rest.
    An' slowly zunk towárd the west
       The evenèn star o' zummer.

In parrock there the haÿ did lie
In weäle below the elems, dry;
An' up in hwome-groun' Jim, that know'd
We all should come along thik road,
'D a-tied the grass in knots that drow'd
    Poor Poll, a-watchèn in the West
    Woone brighter star than all the rest,—
       The evenèn star o' zummer.

The stars that still do zet an' rise,
Did sheen in our forefather's eyes;
They glitt'd to the vu'st men's zight,
The last will have em in their night;
But who can vind em half so bright
   As I thought thik peäle star above
    My smilèn Jeäne, my zweet vu'st love,
      The evenèn star o' zummer.

How sweet's the mornèn fresh an' new,
Wi' sparklèn brooks an' glitt'rèn dew;
How sweet's the noon wi' sheädes a-drow'd
Upon the groun' but leätely mow'd,
An' bloomèn flowers all abrode;
   But sweeter still, as I do clim',
    Theäse woody hill in evenèn dim
      'S the evenèn star o' zummer.

The Clote

(WATER-LILY)

O zummer clote! when the brook's a-slidèn
   So slow an' smooth down his zedgy bed,
Upon thy broad leaves so seäfe a-ridèn
   The water's top wi' thy yoller head.
     By black rin'd allers,
     An' weedy shallers
Thee then dost float, goolden zummer clote!

The grey-bough'd withy's a-leänèn lowly
   Above the water thy leaves do hide;
The bendèn bulrush, a-swaÿèn slowly,
   Do skirt in zummer thy river's zide;
       An' perch in shoals, O,
       Do vill the holes, O,
Where thee dost float, goolden zummer clote!

Oh, when thy brook-drinkèn flow'r 's a-blowèn,
  The burnèn zummer's a-zettèn in;
The time o' greenness, the time o' mowèn,
  When in the haÿ-vield, wi' zunburnt skin,
      The vo'k do drink, O,
      Upon the brink, O,
Where thee dost float, goolden zummer clote!

Wi' eärms a-spreadèn, an' cheäks a-blowèn,
  How proud wer I when I vu'st could zwim
Athirt the deep pleäce where thou bist growèn,
  Wi' thy long more vrom the bottom dim;
      While cows, knee-high, O,
      In brook, wer nigh, O,
Where thee dost float, goolden zummer clote!

Ov all the brooks drough the meäds a-windèn,
  Ov all the meäds by a river's brim,
There's nwone so feäir o' my own heart's vindèn,
  As where the maïdens do zee thee swim,
      An' stan' to teäke, O,
      Wi' long-stemm'd reäke, O,
Thy flow'r afloat, goolden zummer clote!

I got two Vields

  I got two vields, an' I don't ceäre
  What squire mid have a bigger sheäre.
  My little zummerleäze do stratch
  All down the hangèn, to a patch
  O' meäd between a hedge an' rank
  Ov elems, an' a river bank.
  Where yoller clotes, in spreadèn beds
  O' floatèn leaves, do lift their heads
  By bendèn bulrushes an' zedge
      101

A-swaÿèn at the water's edge,
Below the withy that do spread
Athirt the brook his grey-leav'd head.
An' eltrot flowers, milky white,
Do catch the slantèn evenèn light;
An' in the meäple boughs, along
The hedge, do ring the blackbird's zong;
Or in the day, a-vleèn drough
The leafy trees, the whoa'se gookoo
Do zing to mowers that do zet
Their zives on end, an' stan' to whet.
From my wold house among the trees
A lcäne do goo along the leäze
O' yoller gravel, down between
Two mossy banks vor ever green.
An' trees, a-hangèn overhead,
Do hide a trinklèn gully-bed,
A-cover'd by a bridge vor hoss
Or man a-voot to come across.
Zoo wi' my hwomestead, I don't ceäre
What squire mid have a bigger sheäre!

Be'mi'ster

Sweet Be'mi'ster, that bist a-bound
By green an' woody hills all round,
Wi' hedges, reachèn up between
A thousan' vields o' zummer green,
Where elems' lofty heads do drow
Their sheädes vor haÿ-meakers below,
An' wild hedge flow'rs do charm the souls
O' maïdens in their evenèn strolls.

When I o' Zunday nights wi' Jeäne
Do saunter drough a vield or leäne,
Where elder-blossoms be a-spread
Above the eltrot's milk-white head,

102

An' flow'rs o' blackberries do blow
Upon the brembles, white as snow,
To be outdone avore my zight
By Jeän's gaÿ frock o' dazzlèn white;

Oh! then there's nothèn that's 'ithout
Thy hills that I do ho about,—
Noo bigger pleäce, noo gaÿer town,
Beyond thy sweet bells' dyèn soun',
As they do ring, or strike the hour,
At evenèn vrom thy wold red tow'r.
No: shelter still my head, an' keep
My bwones when I do vall asleep.

Jenny out vrom Hwome

O wild-reävèn west winds, as you do roar on,
    The elems do rock an' the poplars do ply,
An' weäve do dreve weäve in the dark-water'd pon',—
    Oh! where do ye rise vrom, an' where do ye die?

O wild-reävèn winds, I do wish I could vlee
    Wi' you, lik' a bird o' the clouds, up above
The rudge o' the hill an' the top o' the tree,
    To where I do long vor, an' vo'kes I do love.

Or else that in under theäse rock I could hear,
    In the soft-zwellèn sounds you do leäve in your road,
Zome words you mid bring me, vrom tongues that be
        dear,
    Vrom friends that do love me, all scatter'd abrode.

O wild-reävèn winds! if you ever do roar
    By the house an' the elems vrom where I'm a-come,
Breathe up at the window, or call at the door,
    An' tell you've a-voun' me a-thinkèn o' hwome.

Night a-Zettèn In

When leäzers wi' their laps o' corn
   Noo longer be a-stoopèn,
An' in the stubble, all vorlorn,
   Noo poppies be a-droopèn;
When theäse young harvest-moon do weäne,
   That now've his horns so thin, O,
We'll leäve off walkèn in the leäne,
   While night's a zettèn in, O.

When zummer doust is all a-laid
   Below our litty shoes, O;
When all the raïn-chill'd flow'rs be dead,
   That now do drink the dews, O;
When beauty's neck, that's now a-show'd,
   'S a-muffled to the chin, O;
We'll leäve off walkèn in the road,
   When night's a-zettèn in, O.

But now, while barley by the road
   Do hang upon the bough, O,
A-pull'd by branches off the lwoad
   A-ridèn hwome to mow, O;
While spiders roun' the flower-stalks
   Ha' cobwebs yet to spin, O,
We'll cool ourzelves in out-door walks,
   When night's a-zettèn in, O.

While down at vword the brook so small,
   That leätely wer so high, O,
Wi' little tinklèn sounds do vall
   In roun' the stwones half dry, O;
While twilight ha' sich aïr in store,
   To cool our zunburnt skin, O,
We'll have a ramble out o' door,
   When night's a-zettèn in, O.

Eclogue

The Common a-Took In

Thomas and John

THOMAS

Good morn t'ye, John. How b'ye? how b'ye?
Zoo you be gwaïn to market, I do zee.
Why, you be quite a-lwoaded wi' your geese.

JOHN

Ees, Thomas, ees.
Why, I'm a-gettèn rid ov ev'ry goose
An' goslèn I've a-got: an' what is woose,
I fear that I must zell my little cow.

THOMAS

How zoo, then, John? Why, what's the matter now?
What, can't ye get along? B'ye run a-ground?
An' can't paÿ twenty shillèns vor a pound?
What, can't ye put a lwoaf on shelf?

JOHN

                    Ees, now;
But I do fear I shan't 'ithout my cow.
No; they do mëan to teäke the moor in, I do hear,
An' 'twill be soon begun upon;
Zoo I must zell my bit o' stock to-year,
Because they woon't have any groun' to run upon.

THOMAS

Why, what d'ye tell o'? I be very zorry
To hear what they be gwaïn about;
But yet I s'pose there'll be a 'lotment vor ye,
When they do come to mark it out.

JOHN

No; not vor me, I fear. An' if there should,
Why, 'twoulden be so handy as 'tis now;
Vor 'tis the common that do do me good,
The run for my vew geese, or vor my cow.

THOMAS

Ees, that's the job; why 'tis a handy thing
To have a bit o' common, I do know,
To put a little cow upon in Spring,
The while woone's bit ov orcha'd grass do grow.

JOHN

Aye, that's the thing, you zee. Now I do mow
My bit o' grass, an' meäke a little rick;
An' in the zummer, while do grow,
My cow do run in common vor to pick
A bleäde or two o' grass, if she can vind em,
Vor tother cattle don't leäve much behind em.
Zoo in the evenèn, we do put a lock
O' nice fresh grass avore the wicket;
An' she do come at vive or zix o'clock,
As constant as the zun, to pick it.
An' then, bezides the cow, why we do let
Our geese run out among the emmet hills;
An' then when we do pluck em, we do get
Vor zeäle zome veathers an' zome quills;
An' in the winter we do fat em well,
An' car em to the market vor to zell
To gentlevo'ks, vor we don't oft avvword
To put a goose a-top ov ouer bwoard;
But we do get our feäst,—vor we be eäble
To clap the giblets up a-top o' teäble.

THOMAS

An' I don't know o' many better things,
Than geese's heads and gizzards, lags an' wings.

JOHN

An' then, when I ha' nothèn else to do,
Why I can teäke my hook an' gloves, an' goo
To cut a lot o' vuzz and briars
Vor hetèn ovens, or vor lightèn viers.
An' when the childern be too young to eärn
A penny, they can g'out in zunny weather,
An' run about, an' get together
A bag o' cow-dung vor to burn.

THOMAS

'Tis handy to live near a common;
But I've a-zeed, an' I've a-zaid,
That if a poor man got a bit o' bread,
They'll try to teäke it vrom en.
But I wer twold back tother day,
That they be got into a way
O' lettèn bits o' groun' out to the poor.

JOHN

Well, I do hope 'tis true, I'm sure;
An' I do hope that they will do it here,
Or I must goo to workhouse, I do fear.

The Happy Days when I wer Young

In happy days when I wer young,
An' had noo ho, an' laugh'd an' zung,
The maïd wer merry by her cow,
An' men wer merry wi' the plough;
But never talk'd, at hwome or out
O' doors, o' what's a-talk'd about
By many now,—that to despise
The laws o' God an' man is wise.

107

Wi' daïly health, an' daïly bread,
An' thatch above their shelter'd head,
They velt noo fear, an' had noo spite,
To keep their eyes awake at night;
But slept in peace wi' God on high
An' man below, an' fit to die.

O' grassy meäd an' woody nook,
An' waters o' the windèn brook,
That sprung below the vu'st dark sky
That raïn'd, to run till seas be dry;
An' hills a-stannèn on while all
The works o' man do rise an' vall;
An' trees the toddlèn child do vind
At vu'st, an' leäve at last behind;
I wish that you could now unvwold
The peace an' jäy o' times o' wold;
An' tell, when death do still my tongue,
O' happy days when I wer young.
Vrom where wer all this venom brought,
To kill our hope an' taïnt our thought?
Clear brook! thy water coulden bring
Such venom vrom thy rocky spring;
Nor could it come in zummer blights,
Or reävèn storms o' winter nights,
Or in the cloud an' viry stroke
O' thunder that do split the woak.

O valley dear! I wish that I
'D a-liv'd in former times, to die
Wi' all the happy souls that trod
Thy turf in peäce, an' died to God;
Or gone wi' them that laugh'd an' zung
In happy days when I wer young!

The Carter

O, I be carter, wi' my whip
  A-smackèn loud, as by my zide,
Up over hill, an' down the dip,
  The heavy lwoad do slowly ride.

An' I do hal in all the crops,
  An' I do bring in vuzz vrom down;
An' I do goo vor wood to copse,
  An' car the corn an' straw to town.

An' I do goo vor lime, an' bring
  Hwome cider wi' my sleek-heäir'd team,
An' smack my limber whip an' zing,
  While all their bells do gaïly cheeme.

An' I do always know the pleäce
  To gi'e the hosses breath, or drug;
An' ev'ry hoss do know my feäce,
  An' mind my *'mether ho*! an' *whog*!

An' merry haÿ-meäkers do ride
  Vrom vield in zummer wi' their prongs,
In my blue waggon, zide by zide
  Upon the reäves, a-zingèn zongs.

An' when the vrost do catch the stream,
  An' oves wi' icicles be hung,
My pantèn hosses' breath do steam
  In white-grass'd vields, a-haulèn dung.

An' mine's the waggon fit vor lwoads,
  An' mine be lwoads to cut a rout;
An' mine's a team, in routy rwoads,
  To pull a lwoaded waggon out.

A zull is nothèn when do come
   Behind their lags; an' they do teäke
A roller as they would a drum,
   An' harrow as they would a reäke.

O! I be a carter, wi' my whip
   A-smackèn loud, as by my zide.
Up over hill, an' down the dip,
   The heavy lwoad do slowly ride.

Lullaby

The rook's nest do rock on the tree-top
Where vew foes can stand;
The martin's is high, an' is deep
In the steep cliff o' zand.
But thou, love, a-sleepèn where vootsteps
Mid come to thy bed,
Hast father an' mother to watch thee
An' shelter thy head.
      Lullaby, Lilybrow.   Lie asleep;
      Blest be thy rest.

An' zome birds do keep under ruffèn
Their young vrom the storm,
An' zome wi' nesthoodèns o' moss
And o' wool, do lie warm.
An' we wull look well to the houseruf
That o'er thee mid leäk,
An' the blast that mid beät on thy winder
Shall not smite thy cheäk.
      Lullaby, Lilibrow.   Lie asleep;
      Blest be thy rest.

The Common a-Took In

Oh! no, Poll, no! Since they've a-took
The common in, our lew wold nook
Don't seem a-bit as used to look
   When we had runnèn room;
Girt banks do shut up ev'ry drong,
An' stratch wi' thorny backs along
Where we did use to run among
The vuzzen an' the broom.

Ees; while the ragged colts did crop
The nibbled grass, I used to hop
The emmetbuts, vrom top to top,
   So proud o' my spry jumps:
Wi' thee behind or at my zide,
A-skippèn on so light an' wide
'S thy little frock would let thee stride,
   Among the vuzzy humps.

An' while the lark up auver head
Did twitter, I did sarch the red
Thick bunch o' broom, or yoller bed
   O' vuzzen vor a nest;
An' thou di'st hunt about, to meet
Wi' strawberries so red an' sweet,
Or clogs or shoes off hosses veet,
   Or wild thyme vor thy breast;

Or when the cows did run about
A-stung, in zummer, by the stout,
Or when they plaÿ'd, or when they foüght,
   Di'st stand a-lookèn on:
An' where white geese, wi' long red bills,
Did veed among the emmet-hills,

There we did goo to vind their quills
   Alongzide o' the pon'.

What fun there wer among us, when
The haÿward come, wi' all his men,
To drève the common, an' to pen
   Strange cattle in the pound;
The cows did bleäre, the men did shout
An' toss their eärms an' sticks about,
An' vo'ks, to own their stock, come out
   Vrom all the housen round.

Easter Bells

The shrunken waters, lately high,
Have left the white-slim'd withies dry,
And pilewort on the bank, holds up
Before the sun its golden cup,
And lightsome-hearted young folk stray
With glossy shoes by ev'ry way,
All happy with their holyday,
   While Easter bells are ringing.

The eastern clouds all fled away
To let the sun rise clear to-day,
And make the high-sky'd world look fair
For joys they meet to-day to share.
So ev'ry youth has gone to find
The maid that's fairest to his mind,
And left his daily work behind
   While Easter bells are ringing.

Our hearts are dull when dark mist flies
Below the gloom of sunless skies,
And beats through leafless trees that yield
No shelter in the wat'ry field;
But gladness stirs our souls at sight
Of gay larks floating in the light
Of blue-sky'd morning, at their height,
   While Easter bells are ringing,—

And blue-wing'd vi'lets lighty shake
In sunny air beside the brake;—
And April's coming on to shed
Her dews upon the cowslip's head;
But this year's flow'rs will all have died
With some now hopeful souls beside,

115

Before another Easter tide
　　Shall come with bells a-ringing.

Rustic Childhood

No city primness train'd my feet
To strut in childhood through the street,
But freedom let them loose to tread
The yellow cowslip's downcast head;
Or climb, above the twining hop
And ivy, to the elm-tree's top;
Where southern airs of blue-sky'd day
Breath'd o'er the daisy and the may.
　　I knew you young, and love you now,
　　　O shining grass, and shady bough.

Far off from town, where splendour tries
To draw the looks of gather'd eyes,
And clocks, unheeded, fail to warn
The loud-tongued party of the morn,
I spent in woodland shades my day
In cheerful work or happy play,
And slept at night where rustling leaves
Threw moonlight shadows o'er my eaves.
　　I knew you young, and love you now,
　　　O shining grass, and shady bough.

Or in the grassy drove by ranks
Of white-stemm'd ashes or by banks
Of narrow lanes, in-winding round
The hedgy sides of shelving ground;
Where low-shot light struck in to end
Again at some cool-shaded bend,
Where we might see through darkleav'd boughs
The evening light on green hill-brows.
　　I knew you young, and love you now,
　　　O shining grass, and shady bough.

116

Or on the hillock where I lay
At rest on some bright holyday;
When short noon-shadows lay below
The thorn in blossom white as snow;
And warm air bent the glist'ning tops
Of bushes in the lowland copse,
Before the blue hills swelling high
And far against the southern sky.
   I knew you young, and love you now,
    O shining grass, and shady bough.

Sonnet: Leaves

Leaves of the summer, lovely summer's pride,
  Sweet is the shade below your silent tree,
Whether in waving copses, where ye hide
  My roamings, or in fields that let me see
  The open sky; and whether ye may be
Around the low-stemm'd oak, robust and wide;
Or taper ash upon the mountain side;
  Or lowland elm; your shade is sweet to me.

Whether ye wave above the early flow'rs
  In lively green; or whether, rustling sere,
Ye fly on playful winds, around my feet,

In dying autumn; lovely are your bow'rs,
  Ye early-dying children of the year;
    Holy the silence of your calm retreat.

Sonnet: Rural Nature

Ye airs of sunny spring that softly blow
  With whisp'ry breathings o'er the grasses' blade,
  Ye grass-bespangling flow'rs—too soon to fade—

That now in gemlike brightness round me grow:
  Ye saplings, and ye greenbough'd trees, that throw
Your waving shadows on the sunny glade;
  Thou lowland stream, whose winding waters flow,
Like molten silver, to the hoarse cascade:

Give vice the noisy town; and let the great
  Ride mighty o'er the earth with pride and pow'r,
Give avarice his gold; but let me flee

Where cold and selfish hearts live not to hate
  And scorn. Oh take me to thy lonely bow'r,
Sweet rural nature! Life is dear for thee.

Whitburn's Green and White

How fresh the air, how soft the light,
That fann'd the cheeks and fill'd the sight,
When *Robert*, in the evening, met
His *Jane* before the sun had set,
Or gath'ring dews had fall'n to wet
The jasmine by the house's side,
Or dark'ning twilight came to hide
        From his fond sight,
        In airy night,
Sweet Whitburn water's green and white.

For climbing plants with flow'rs and leaves
Hid all the wall from ground to eaves;
And stems of snow-white lilies plied,
Wind-shaken, by the lawn spread wide
And long before the house's side;
And snow-white geese, with quiv'ring tails,
Were cackling by the snow-white rails,
        And filled the sight,
        In summer light,
With lively hues of green and white.

(IN NATIONAL ENGLISH)

A snow-white bridge of trusty planks
Bore Robert o'er the brook's green banks,
Above the ribbon'd sedge's stalk,
And water sparkling on the chalk;
And when young Jenny took her walk
On Sunday evenings, in the height
Of summer, she was all in white;
  And walk'd in mien
  A stately queen,
In Whitburn water's white and green.

The appletrees with snow-white bloom
O'erspread the grassy orchard's gloom,
And hawthorns open'd to the heat
In ev'ry hedge, their snow-white sheet;
And where she walk'd with light-shod feet,
The daisy-buds, not yet conceal'd
By grass, bespangled all the field;
  While May's warm light,
  Had thus bedight,
All Whitburn with its green and white.

But Robert had to go away
From Jenny, on from June till May;
And coming back he found her wan,
With black instead of white put on
For both the old folk that were gone,
And underneath their grassy heap
And chalk-white headstone lay asleep;
  Betok'ning right,
  To others' sight,
Their love of Whitburn's green and white.

But they, poor souls, could only save
Enough to take them to the grave,
And so left Jane, with tearful pray'r,
Behind, to God's unfailing care.

But Robert took her soon to share
The joys and trials of his life,
His everfaithful-hearted wife,
    So dear's the light,
    To his fond sight,
For olden days of green and white.

And so he went away and took
The little farm at Whitburn brook;
And train'd the jasmine round the door,
And kept the green as 'twas before,
With all the railings painted o'er
Snow-white, and red-legg'd geese to swim
The stream, or tread its weedy brim;
    That so the light,
    May give his sight,
Dear Whitburn's hues of green and white.

'How Sweet's the Love that meets Return'

One glowing evening, when shades were dark'ning
   Below the elm trees before her door,
I pass'd with light ling'ring footsteps, hark'ning
   To sounds that struck through my fond heart's core.
For there, with soul-touching turn and swell,
An unknown voice sweetly rose and fell,
And sang, as far as I then could learn,
'How sweet's the love that meets return'.

There in the hall by the evening lighted
   Within a casement set open wide,
And tired with work that she never slighted,
   She sat at rest by her brother's side;
And, as the tune wound so high and low,
Beneath his light string-awak'ning bow,
She sang the old song she wish'd to learn,
'How sweet's the love that meets return'.

120

And once I saw her so light's a fairy,
   With glowing cheeks under glossy locks,
With busy hands cutting down rosemary,
   And blue-ear'd spike for her snow-white frocks
And felt that no one of womankind
Could take like her my bewildered mind,
I lov'd her fondly, but had to learn
'How sweet's the love that meets return'.

But when at Maypole we young folk parted
   Below the garlands with dying leaves,
And I took her off, so happy-hearted
   To see her home to her house's eaves;
Then by the kind words she spoke so fast,
And by her looks and her smiles at last,
I found that night, by the moon-bright durn,
'How sweet's the love that meets return'.

And when for my sake, in wedlock holy,
   She left the old folks to sit alone,
While through the evening the clock tick'd slowly,
   And crickets chirp'd by the warm hearth-stone;
They lov'd to talk of their daughter gone,
And wondered how we were going on;
For in their hearts never ceased to burn
For her, the love that met return.

And when, soon after, again I drove her
   Back home to see them, a welcome child,
She laugh'd to see how her flow'rs ran over
   The place, forsaken and rambling wild.
Within her room one had dared to peep,
As though to see if she lay asleep,
And some climbed over the pales and durn,
As if in love that sought return.

The Lane

I love the narrow lane's dark bows,
When summer glows or winter blows;
Or when the hedge-born primrose hides
Its head upon the dry bankside,
By ribby-rinded maple shoots,
Or round the dark-stemm'd hazel's roots;
Where weather-beaten ivy winds
Unwith'ring o'er the elms' brown rinds,
And where the ash's white bough whips
The whistling air with coal-black tips;
And where the grassy ground, beside
The gravel-washing brook, lies wide,
And leaping lambs, with shrill-toned throats,
Bleat loudly in their first white coats,
And rooks through clear air cleave, in black
And cloud-high flocks, their unmark'd track,
And merry larks are whistling loud,
Aloft, unshaded by a cloud.

I like the narrow lane's dark bows,
When winter blows or summer glows;
Where under summer suns, between
The sappy boughs of lively green,
The playful shadows mutely mock
The moving trees that breezes rock,
And robinhoods bloom red below
The rough-stemm'd bramble's flow'ry bow,
And stitchwort's bending stalks upbear
Their starlike cups to sultry air,
Where I may hear the wind-brought words
Of workfolk, with the songs of birds,
And rubb'd scythes reared upon their sneads,
And ringing in the roadside meads.

I love the narrow lane's dark bows,
When summer glows or winter blows;
Or in the *f*all, when leaves all *f*ade,
Yet *f*lutt'ring in the airy shade,
And in the *sh*elter'd *sh*aw the blast
Has *sh*aken down the green-cupp'd mast,
And time is *bl*ack'ning *bl*ue-skinn'd sloes,
And *bl*ackberries on bramble bows,
And *r*ipening haws are growing *r*ed
A*r*ound the grey-rin'd hawthorn's head,
And hazel *br*anches, *br*okentipp'd
And *br*own, of all their nuts are stripp'd,
And in the leazes, *wh*iffling *wh*ite,
The *wh*irling thistle seeds alight
In sunshine, *st*ruck from bents' brown *st*alks
By *st*rolling girls in Sunday walks.

I love the narrow lane's dark bows,
When summer glows or winter blows,
And *w*ildly driven *w*et is cast
Through *w*indy gates upon the blast,
And *tr*ickling down the *tr*ees, around
Their *tr*unks, the rain drops fall to ground,
And *w*ither'd leaves, too *w*et to ride
The *w*inds, line ev'ry ditches side,
Nor *s*ongs of birds, nor merry *s*ounds,
Of *s*ouls at work are in the grounds:
O then the *l*ane affords its *l*ee
Of *l*imber bough, and sturdy tree,
And so I love its winding bows
When summer glows or winter blows.

A Winter Night

It was a chilly winter's night;
   And frost was glitt'ring on the ground,
And evening stars were twinkling bright;
   And from the gloomy plain around
      Came no sound,
But where, within the wood-girt tow'r,
The churchbell slowly struck the hour;

As if that all of human birth
   Had risen to the final day,
And soaring from the wornout earth
   Were called in hurry and dismay,
      Far away;
And I alone of all mankind
Were left in loneliness behind.

Moss

O rain-bred moss that now dost hide
The timber's bark and wet rock's side,
Upshining to the sun, between
The darksome storms, in lively green,
And wash'd by pearly rain drops clean,
   Steal o'er my lonely path, and climb
   My wall, dear child of silent time.
      O winter moss, creep on, creep on,
      And warn me of the time that's gone.

Green child of winter, born to take
Whate'er the hands of man forsake,
That makest dull, in rainy air,

124

His labour-brighten'd works; so fair
While newly left in summer's glare;
　And stealest o'er the stone that keeps
　His name in mem'ry where he sleeps.
　　O winter moss, creep on, creep on,
　　And warn us of the time that's gone.

Come, lowly plant that lov'st, like me,
The shadow of the woodland tree,
And waterfall where echo mocks
The milkmaid's song by dripping rocks,
And sunny turf for roving flocks,
　And ribby elms extending wide
　Their roots within the hillock's side.
　　Come, winter moss, creep on, creep on,
　　And warn me of the time that's gone.

Come, meet me wandering, and call
My mind to some green mould'ring hall
That once stood high, the fair-wall'd pride
Of hearts that lov'd, and hoped, and died,
Ere thou hadst climb'd around its side:
　Where blooming faces once were gay
　For eyes no more to know the day.
　　Come, winter moss, creep on, creep on
　　And warn me of the time that's gone.

While there in youth,—the sweetest part
Of life,—with joy-believing heart,
They liv'd their own dear days, all fraught
With incidents for after-thought
In later life, when fancy brought
　The outline of some faded face
　Again to its forsaken place.
　　Come, winter moss, creep on, creep on,
　　And warn me of the time that's gone.

Come where thou climbedst, fresh and free,
The grass-beglooming apple-tree,
That, hardly shaken with my small
Boy's strength, with quiv'ring head, let fall
The apples we lik'd most of all,
  Or elm I climb'd, with clasping legs,
  To reach the crow's high-nested eggs.
    Come, winter moss, creep on, creep on,
    And warn me of the time that's gone.

Or where I found thy yellow bed
Below the hill-borne fir-tree's head,
And heard the whistling east wind blow
Above, while wood-screen'd down below
I rambled in the spring-day's glow,
  And watch'd the low-ear'd hares upspring
  From cover, and the birds take wing.
    Come, winter moss, creep on, creep on,
    And warn me of the time that's gone.

Or where the bluebells bent their tops
In windless shadows of the copse;
Or where the misty westwind blew
O'er primroses that peer'd out through
Thy bankside bed, and scatter'd dew
  O'er grey spring grass I watch'd alone
  Where thou hadst grown o'er some old stone.
    Come, winter moss, creep on, creep on,
    And warn me of the time that's gone.

Burncombe Hollow

While snowy nightwinds, blowing bleak
Up hill, made rock-borne fir-trees creak,
And drove the snow-flakes, feather-light,

126

O'er icy streams in playsome flight,
And while the roof was snowy white,
　　There blazing cleftwood threw its heat
　　With ruddy light, to chilly feet,
　　　　In lonely Burncombe hollow.

And Jenny, that had just put down
Her load of errands brought from town,
Sat leaning backward in her chair,
Cheek-warm, with weather-loosen'd hair;
And told, with smiles 'twas bliss to share,
　　Her news; while putting out for heat,
　　Down side by side, her comely feet,
　　　　At home in Burncombe hollow.

And while the children ran to pull
Her errands from her basket full,
Her friends and I, all wordless, hung
Upon the words of her gay tongue;
But they with old love, I with young,
　　For all my soul, with all my sight,
　　Were given up that happy night,
　　　　To Jane of Burncombe hollow.

And where did first her sweet voice own
Her love for me and me alone,
But climbing up the eastern side
Of Burncombe hollow, that did hide
The western sunset, crimson-dyed,
　　O'er leaves that rustled on the ground,
　　Below the ivy twining round
　　　　The trees of Burncombe hollow.

And now her careful friends that bred,
Her up so fair and good, are dead;
And she, a woman mild and staid,
Is keeping house where once she play'd

And won my love, a blooming maid;
  And all the joy my soul can know
  With her will stay, with her must go
    From me in Burncombe hollow.

And so 'tis sweet with her my wife
To look back o'er our wedded life,
Which she, e'er smiling in my sight,
Has made a cloudless day, still bright,
But waning slowly into night;
  And if I had my time once more
  To choose, I'd choose no maid before
    The maid of Burncombe hollow.

So winter darkness come to brood
O'er sullen moans of waving wood,
Come hov'ring snow, so lightly cast
Upon the ground where ice seals fast
The water from the cutting blast.
  I heed you not, while shelter'd where
  Love lights me up the ruddy glare
    Of fire in Burncombe hollow.

Mary comes not to the Tree

Ye clouds that *h*ide, with *h*asty flight,
The *h*igh-gone moon's inconstant light;
Ye *r*oaring nightwinds, flitting *r*ound
The *r*ocking tree with hollow sound,
While *d*ashing *d*own the scatter'd *d*rops
Of *d*riven rain from high boughtops,
A darksome night ye *m*ake for *m*e,
For *M*ary comes not to the tree.

For *w*at'ry grass now *w*aves its head
Too *w*et for her light feet to tread
128

And *br*imful *br*ooks, that wildly roll
Out*br*eaking from their banks' controul,
In ruffled sheets, are *w*ashing *w*ide
The *w*illows by the water side,
In *fl*oods o'er*fl*owing, like a sea,
Her *f*ootway over to the tree.

I *s*aw her *s*oft looks out before
The *s*un this morning at the door,
To see the *fl*ail, with *fl*ying staff,
Swing *fl*eetly round, and fan-blown chaff
Sink *f*eather light in hov'ring *f*alls
Be*f*ore the old barn's moss-green walls,
And *t*ook her *t*oken she would be
In *t*ime to night below the tree.

So *sp*end, ye raving storms, your *sp*ite
In *sp*eed upon the earth to night;
Ye *w*avy *w*aters roll away
Ere *w*anes another longsome day,
That moonspread *l*ight may *l*ure once more
My *l*ovely Mary from her door,
And *s*oftly *s*hine to let her see
Her *s*afest footway to the tree.

Sonnet: To a Garden, on leaving it

Sweet garden! peaceful spot! no more in thee
   Shall I e'er while away the sunny hour.
Farewell each blooming shrub, and lofty tree;
   Farewell the mossy path and nodding flow'r:
   I shall not hear again from yonder bow'r
The song of birds, or humming of the bee,
Nor listen to the waterfall, nor see
   The clouds float on behind the lofty tow'r.

No more, at breezy eve, or dewy morn,
  My gliding scythe shall shear thy mossy green:
My busy hands shall never more adorn,

  My eyes no more may see, this peaceful scene.
But still, sweet spot, wherever I may be,
My love-led soul will wander back to thee.

Sonnet: Architecture

O noble art! how greatly I delight
  In noble works of thy gigantic hand!
  The lofty columns' massy shafts, that stand
Beneath entablatures of stately height;
The tap'ring spire that reaches out of sight;
  The lofty roof; with arches that expand
  To dumb-beholden width; and windows grand
And glorious with many-colour'd light!

O noble art! how long thy works out-dwell
  The sons of men! The piles that linger still
  In early-citied Egypt's rainless clime,

And on the holy soil of Greece, will tell
  How masterly thou workest, since thy skill
  Can mock the working of all-wasting time.

My Orcha'd in Linden Lea

'Ithin the woodlands, flow'ry gleäded,
    By the woak tree's mossy moot,
The sheenèn grass-bleädes, timber-sheäded,
    Now do quiver under voot;
An' birds do whissle auver head,
An' water's bubblèn in its bed,
An' there vor me the apple tree
Do leän down low in Linden Lea.

When leaves that leätely wer a-springèn
    Now do feäde 'ithin the copse,
An' painted birds do hush their zingèn
    Up upon the timber's tops;
An' brown-leav'd fruit's a-turnèn red,
In cloudless zunsheen, auver head,
Wi' fruit vor me, the apple tree
Do leän down low in Linden Lea.

Let other vo'k meäke money vaster
    In the aïr o' dark-room'd towns,
I don't dread a peevish meäster;
    Though noo man do heed my frowns,
I be free to goo abrode,
Or teäke my hwomeward road
To where, vor me, the apple tree
Do leän down low in Linden Lea.

Day's Work a-Done

And oh! the jaÿ our rest did yield,
  At evenèn by the mossy wall,
When we'd a-work'd all day a-vield,
   While zummer zuns did rise an' vall,
     As there a-lettèn
     Goo all frettèn,
An' vorgettèn all our twiles,
We zot among our childern's smiles.

An' under skies that glitter'd white,
  The while our smoke, arisèn blue,
Did melt in aïer, out o' zight,
   Above the trees that kept us lew;
     Wer birds a-zingèn,
     Tongues a-ringèn,
Childern springèn, vull o' jaÿ,
A-finishèn the day in plaÿ.

An' back behind, a-stannèn tall,
  The cliff did sheen to western light;
An' while avore the water-vall,
   A-rottlèn loud, an' foamèn white.
     The leaves did quiver,
     Gnots did whiver,
By the river, where the pool,
In evenèn aïr did glissen cool.

An' childern there, a-runnèn wide,
  Did plaÿ their geämes along the grove,
Vor though to us 'twer jaÿ to bide
   At rest, to them 'twer jaÿ to move.
     The while my smilèn
     Jeäne, beguilèn,
All my twilèn, wi' her ceäre,
Did call me to my evenèn feäre.

The Waggon a-Stooded

Dree o'm a-ta'kèn o't.

(1) Well, here we be, then, wi' the vu'st poor lwoad
O' vuzz we brought, a-stoodèd in the road.

(2) The road, George, no. There's na'r a road   That's
wrong.
If we'd a road, we mid ha' got along.

(1) Noo road! Ees 'tis, the road that we do goo.

(2) Do goo, George, no. The pleäce we can't get
drough.

(1) Well, there, the vu'st lwoad we 've a-haul'd to day
Is here a-stoodèd in theäse bed o' clay.
Here's rotten groun'! an' how the wheels do cut!
The little woone's a-zunk up to the nut.

(3) An' yeet this rotten groun' don't reach a lug.

(1) Well, come, then, gi'e the plow another tug.

(2) They meäres wull never pull the waggon out,
A-lwoaded, an' a-stoodèd in thik rout.

(3) We'll try.Come, *Smiler*, come! C' up, *Whitevoot*,
gee!

(2) White-voot wi' lags all auver mud! Hee! Hee!

(3) 'Twoon't wag. We shall but snap our gear,
An' overstrain the meäres. 'Twoon't wag, 'tis clear.

135

(1) That's your work, William. No, in coo'se, 'twoon't
   wag.
   Why did ye drēve en into theäse here quag?
   The vore-wheels be a-zunk above the nuts.

(3) What then? I coulden leäve the beäten track,
   To turn the waggon auver on the back
   Ov woone o' theäsem wheel-high emmet-butts.
   If you be sich a drēver, an' do know't,
   You drēve the plow, then; but you'll auverdrow 't.

(1) I drēve the plow, indeed! Oh! ees, what, now
   The wheels woont wag, then, *I* mid drēve the plow!
   We'd better dig away the groun' below
   The wheels. (2) There's na'r a speäde to dig wi'.

(1) An' teäke an' cut a lock o' frith, an' drow
   Upon the clay. (2) Nor hook to cut a twig wi'.

(1) Oh! here's a bwoy a-comèn. Here, my lad,
   Dost know vor a'r a speäde, that can be had?

(B) At father's. (1) Well, where's that? (Bwoy) At
   Sam'el Riddick's.

(1) Well run, an' ax vor woone. Fling up your heels,
   An' mind: a speäde to dig out theäsem wheels,
   An' hook to cut a little lock o' widdicks.

(3) Why, we shall want zix ho'ses, or a dozen,
   To pull the waggon out, wi' all theäse vuzzen.

(1) Well, we mus' lighten en; come, Jeämes, then, hop
   Upon the lwoad, an' jus' fling off the top.

(2) If I can clim' en; but 'tis my consaït,
   That I shall auverzet en wi' my waïght.

(1) You auverzet en! No, Jeämes, he won't vall,
   The lwoad's a-built so firm as any wall.

(2) Here! lend a hand or shoulder vor my knee
   Or voot. I'll scramble to the top an' zee
   What I can do. Well, here I be, among
   The fakkets, vor a bit, but not vor long.
   Heigh, George! Ha! ha! Why this wull never stand.
   Your firm 's a wall, is all so loose as zand;
   'Tis all a-come to pieces. Oh! Teäke ceäre!
   Ho! I'm a-vallèn, vuzz an' all! Haë! There!

(1) Lo'k there, thik fellor is a-vell lik' lead,
   An' half the fuzzen wi 'n, heels over head!
   There's all the vuzz a-lyèn lik' a staddle,
   An' he a-deäb'd wi' mud. Oh! Here's a caddle!

(3) An' zoo you soon got down zome vuzzen, Jimmy.

(2) Ees, I do know 'tis down, I brought it wi' me.

(3) Your lwoad, George, wer a rather slick-built thing,
   But there, 'twer prickly vor the hands! Did sting?

(1) Oh! ees, d'ye teäke me vor a nincompoop,
   No, no. The lwoad wer up so firm 's a rock,
   But two o' theäsem emmet-butts would knock
   The tightest barrel nearly out o' hoop.

(3) Oh! now then, here's the bwoy a-bringèn back
   The speäde. Well done, my man. That idden slack.

(2) Well done, my lad, sha't have a ho'se to ride
   When thou'st a meäre. (Bwoy) Next never's-tide.

(3) Now let's dig out a spit or two
   O' clay, a-vore the little wheels;
   Oh! so's, I can't pull up my heels,
   I be a-stogg'd up over shoe.

(1) Come, William, dig away! Why do you spuddle
    A'most so weak's a child. How you do muddle!
    Gi'e me the speäde a-bit. A pig would rout
    It out a'most so nimbly wi' his snout.

(3) Oh! so's, d'ye hear it, then. How we can thunder!
    How big we be, then George! what next I wonder?

(1) Now, William, gi'e the waggon woone mwore
      twitch,
    The wheels be free, an' 'tis a lighter nitch.

(3) Come, *Smiler*, gee! C'up, *White-voot*. (1) That wull
    do

(2) Do wag. (1) Do goo at last. (3) Well done. 'Tis
    drough.

(1) Now, William, till you have mwore ho'ses' lags,
    Don't drēve the waggon into theäsem quags.

(3) You build your lwoads up tight enough to ride.

(1) I can't do less, d'ye know, wi' you vor guide.

The Young that died in Beauty

If souls should only sheen so bright
In heaven as in e'thly light,
An' nothèn better wer the ceäse,
How comely still, in sheäpe an' feäce,
Would many reach thik happy pleäce,—
The hopeful souls that in their prime
Ha' seem'd a-took avore their time—
The young that died in beauty.

But when woone's lim's ha' lost their strangth
A-twilèn drough a lifetime's langth,
An' auver cheäks a-growèn wold
The slowly-weästen years ha' rolled,
The deep'nèn wrinkle's hollor vwold;
When life is ripe, then death do call
Vor less ov thought, than when do vall
On young vo'ks in their beauty.

But pinèn souls, wi' heads a-hung
In heavy sorrow vor the young,
The sister or the brother dead,
The father wi' a child a-vled,
The husband when his bride ha' laid
Her head at rest, noo mwore to turn,
Have all a-vound the time to murn
Vor youth that died in beauty.

An' yeet the church, where praÿer do rise
Vrom thoughtvul souls, wi' downcast eyes,
An' village greens, a-beät half beäre
By dancers that do meet, an' weär
Such merry looks at feäst an' feäir,
Do gather under leätest skies,
Their bloomèn cheäks an' sparklèn eyes,
Though young ha' died in beauty.

But still the dead shall mwore than keep
The beauty ov their eärly sleep;
Where comely looks shall never weär
Uncomely, under twile an' ceäre.
The feär at death be always feäir,
Still feäir to livers' thought an' love,
An' feäirer still to God above,
Than when they died in beauty.

Our Abode in Arby Wood

Though ice do hang upon the willows
    Out bezide the vrozen brook,
An' storms do roar above our pillows,
    Drough the night, 'ithin our nook;
Our evenèn he'th's a-glowèn warm,
    Drough wringèn vrost, an' roarèn storm.
Though winds mid meäke the wold beams she äke.
    In our abode in Arby Wood.

An' there, though we mid hear the timber
    Creake avore the windy raïn;
An' climèn ivy quiver, limber,
    Up ageän the window peäne;
Our merry vaïces then do sound,
    In rollèn glee, or dree-vaïce round;
Though wind mid roar, 'ithout the door,
    Ov our abode in Arby Wood.

The Wold Wall

Here, Jeäne, we vu'st did meet below
The leafy boughs, a-swingèn slow,
Avore the zun, wi' evenèn glow,
Above our road, a-beamèn red;
The grass in zwath wer in the meäds,
The water gleam'd among the reeds
In aïr a-steälèn roun' the hall,
Where ivy clung upon the wall.
Ah! well-a-day! O wall adieu!
The wall is wold, my grief is new.

An' there you walk'd wi' blushèn pride,
Where softly-wheelèn streams did glide,
Drough sheädes o' poplars at my zide,
An' there wi' love that still do live,
Your feäce did wear the smile o' youth,
The while you spoke wi' age's truth,
An' wi' a rwosebud's mossy ball,
I deck'd your bosom vrom the wall.
Ah! well-a-day! O wall adieu!
The wall is wold, my grief is new.

But now when winter's raïn do vall,
An' wind do beät ageän the hall,
The while upon the wat'ry wall
In spots o' grey the moss do grow;
The ruf noo mwore shall auverspread
The pillor ov our weary head,
Nor shall the rwose's mossy ball
Behang vor you the house's wall.
Ah! well-a-day! O wall adieu!
The wall is wold, my grief is new.

John Bleäke at Hwome at Night

No: where the woak do auverspread,
The grass begloom'd below his head,
An' water, under bowèn zedge,
A-springèn vrom the river's edge,
Do ripple, as the win' do blow,
An' sparkle, as the sky do glow;
An' grey-leav'd withy-boughs do cool,
Wi' darksome sheädes, the clear-feäced pool,
My chimny smoke, 'ithin the lew
O' trees is there arisèn blue;
Avore the night do dim our zight,
Or candle-light, a-sheenèn bright,
Do sparkle drough the window.

When crumpled leaves o' Fall do bound
Avore the wind, along the ground,
An' wither'd bennet-stems do stand
A-quiv'rèn on the chilly land;
The while the zun, wi' zettèn rim,
Do leäve the workman's pathway dim;
An' sweet-breath'd childern's hangèn heads
Be laid wi' kisses, on their beds;
Then I do seek my woodland nest,
An' zit bezide my vier at rest,
While night's a-spread, where day's a-vled,
An' lights do shed their beams o' red,
A-sparklèn drough the window.

If winter's whistlèn winds do vreeze
The snow a-gather'd on the trees,
An' sheädes o' poplar stems do vall
In moonlight up athirt the wall;
An' icicles do hang below
The oves, a-glitt'rèn in a row,
An' risèn stars do slowly ride
Above the ruf's upslantèn zide;
Then I do lay my weary head
Asleep upon my peaceful bed,
When middle-night ha' quench'd the light
Ov embers bright, an' candles white
A-beamèn drough the window.

Zun-zet

Where the western zun, unclouded,
  Up above the grey hill-tops,
Did sheen drough ashes, lofty sh'ouded.
  On the turf bezide the copse,
    In zummer weather,
    We together,

142

Sorrow-slightèn, work-vorgettèn.
Gambol'd wi' the zun a-zetten.

There, by flow'ry bows o' bramble,
    Under hedge, in ash-tree sheädes,
The dun-heaïr'd ho'se did slowly ramble
    On the grasses' dewy bleädes,
        Zet free o' lwoads,
        An' stwony rwoads,
        Vorgetvul o' the lashes frettèn,
        Grazèn wi' the zun a-zettèn.

There wer rooks a-beätèn by us
    Drough the aïr, in a vlock,
An' there the lively blackbird, nigh us,
    On the meäple bough did rock,
        Wi' ringèn droat,
        Where zunlight smote
        The yollow boughs o' zunny hedges
        Auver western hills' blue edges.

Waters, drough the meäds a-purlèn,
    Glissen'd in the evenèn's light,
An' smoke, above the town a-curlèn,
    Melted slowly out o' zight;
        An' there, in glooms
        Ov unzunn'd rooms,
        To zome, wi' idle sorrows frettèn,
        Zuns did set avore their zettèn.

We were out in geämes and reäces,
    Loud a-laughèn, wild in me'th,
Wi' windblown heäir, an' zunbrown'd feäces,
    Leäpen on the high-sky'd e'th,
        Avore the lights
        Wer tin'd o' nights,
        An' while the gossamer's light nettèn
        Sparkled to the zun a-zettèn.

143

The Water Crowvoot

O small-feäc'd flow'r that now dost bloom
To stud wi' white the shallor Frome,
An' leäve the clote to spread his flow'r
On darksome pools o' stwoneless Stour,
When sof'ly-rizèn aïrs do cool
The water in the sheenèn pool,
Thy beds o' snow-white buds do gleam
So feäir upon the sky-blue stream,
As whitest clouds, a-hangèn high
Avore the blueness o' the sky;
An' there, at hand, the thin-heäir'd cows,
In aïry sheädes o' withy boughs,
Or up bezide the mossy raïls,
Do stan' an' zwing their heavy taïls,
The while the ripplèn stream do flow
Below the dousty bridge's bow;
An' quiv'rèn water-gleams do mock
The weäves, upon the sheäded rock;
An' up athirt the copèn stwone
The laïtren bwoy do leän alwone,
A-watchèn, wi' a stedvast look,
The vallèn waters in the brook,
The while the zand o' time do run
An' leäve his errand still undone.
An' oh! as long's thy buds would gleam
Above the softly-slidèn stream,
While sparklèn zummer-brooks do run
Below the lofty-climèn zun,
I only wish that thou could'st staÿ
Vor noo man's harm, an' all men's jaÿ.
But no, the waterman 'ull weäde
Thy water wi' his deadly bleäde,
To slay thee even in thy bloom,
Fair small-feäced flower o' the Frome.

The Lilac

Dear lilac-tree, a-spreadèn wide
Thy purple blooth on ev'ry zide,
As if the hollow sky did shed
Its blue upon thy flow'ry head;
Oh! whether I mid sheäre wi' thee
Thy open aïr, my bloomèn tree,
Or zee thy blossoms vrom the gloom,
'Ithin my zunless workèn-room,
My heart do leäp, but leäp wi' sighs,
At zight o' thee avore my eyes,
For when thy grey-blue head do swaÿ
In cloudless light, 'tis Spring, 'tis Maÿ.

'Tis Spring, 'tis Maÿ, as Maÿ woonce shed
His glowèn light above thy head—
When thy green boughs, wi' bloomy tips,
Did sheäde my childern's laughèn lips;
A-screenèn vrom the noonday gleäre
Their rwosy cheäks an' glossy heäir;
The while their mother's needle sped,
Too quick vor zight, the snow-white thread,
Unless her han', wi' lovèn ceäre,
Did smooth their little heads o' heäir;

Or wi' a sheäke, tie up anew
Vor zome wild voot, a slippèn shoe;
An' I did leän bezide thy mound
Ageän the deäsy-dappled ground,
The while the woaken clock did tick
My hour o' rest away too quick,
An' call me off to work anew,
Wi' slowly-ringèn strokes, woone, two.
Zoo let me zee noo darksome cloud
Bedim to-day thy flow'ry sh'oud,

But let en bloom on ev'ry spraÿ,
Drough all the days o' zunny Maÿ.

Wayfearen

The sky wer clear, the zunsheen glow'd
    On droopèn flowers drough the day,
As I did beät the dousty road
    Vrom hinder hills, a-feädèn gray;
    Drough hollows up the hills,
    Vrom knaps along by mills,
Vrom mills by churches tow'rs, wi' bells
    That twold the hours to woody dells.

An' when the windèn road do guide
    The thirsty vootman where mid flow
The water vrom a rock bezide
    His vootsteps, in a sheenèn bow;
    The hand a-hollow'd up
    Do beät a goolden cup,
To catch an' drink it, bright an' cool,
A-vallèn light 'ithin the pool.

Zoo when, at last, I hung my head
    Wi' thirsty lips a-burnèn dry,
I come bezide a river-bed
    Where water flow'd so blue's the sky;
    An' there I meäde me up
    O' coltsvoot leaf a cup,
Where water vrom his lip o' gray,
Wer sweet to sip thik burnèn day.

But when our work is right, a jaÿ
    Do come to bless us in its traïn,
An' hardships ha' zome good to paÿ
    The thoughtvul soul vor all their päin:

The het do sweetèn sheäde,
 An' weary lim's ha' meäde
A bed o' slumber, still an' sound,
By woody hill or grassy mound.

An' while I zot in sweet delaÿ
 Below an elem on a hill,
Where boughs a-halfwaÿ up did swaÿ
 In sheädes o' lim's above em still,
 An' blue sky show'd between
 The flutt'rèn leäves o' green;
I woulden gi'e that gloom an' sheäde
Vor any room that weälth ha' meäde.

But oh! that vo'k that have the roads
 Where weary-vooted souls do pass,
Would leäve bezide the stwone vor lwoads,
 A little strip vor zummer grass;
 That when the stwones do bruise
 An' burn an' gall our tooes,
We then mid cool our veet on beds
O' wild-thyme sweet, or deäisy-heads.

The Leäne

They do zay that a travellèn chap
 Have a-put in the newspeäper now,
That the bit o' green ground on the knap
 Should be all a-took in vor the plough.
He do fancy 'tis easy to show
 That we can be but stunpolls at best,
Vor to leäve a green spot where a flower can grow,
 Or a voot-weary walker mid rest.
'Tis hedge-grubbèn, Thomas, an' ledge-grubbèn,
  Never a-done
While a sov'rèn mwore's to be won.

147

The road, he do zay, is so wide
　　As 'tis wanted vor travellers' wheels,
As if all that did travel did ride
　　An' did never get galls on their heels.
He would leäve sich a thin strip o' groun',
　　That, if a man's veet in his shoes
Wer a-burnèn an' zore, why he coulden zit down
　　But the wheels would run over his tooes.
Vor 'tis meäke money, Thomas, an' teäke money,
　　　　What's zwold an' bought
Is all that is worthy o' thought.

Years agoo the leäne-zides did bear grass,
　　Vor to pull wi' the geeses' red bills,
That did hiss at the vo'k that did pass,
　　Or the bwoys that pick'd up their white quills.
But shortly, if vower or vive
　　Ov our goslèns do creep vrom the agg,
They must mwope in the geärden, mwore dead than
　　　alive,
　　In a coop, or a-tied by the lag.
Vor to catch at land, Thomas, an' snatch at land,
　　　　Now is the plan;
Meäke money wherever you can.

The childern wull soon have noo pleäce
　　Vor to plaÿ in, an' if they do grow,
They wull have a thin musheroom feäce,
　　Wi' their bodies so sumple as dough.
But a man is a-meäde ov a child,
　　An' his limbs do grow worksome by plaÿ;
An' if the young child's little body's a-spweil'd,
　　Why, the man's wull the sooner decay.
But wealth is wo'th now mwore than health is wo'th;
　　　　Let it all goo,
If't 'ull bring but a sov'rèn or two.

148

Vor to breed the young fox or the heäre,
    We can gi'e up whole eäcres o' ground,
But the greens be a-grudg'd, vor to rear
    Our young childern up healthy an' sound,
Why, there woont be a-left the next age
    A green spot where their veet can goo free;
An' the goocoo wull soon be committed to cage
    Vor a trespass in zomebody's tree.
Vor 'tis lockèn up, Thomas, an' blockèn up,
        Stranger or brother,
Men mussen come nigh woone another.

Woone day I went in at a geäte,
    Wi' my child, where an echo did sound,
An' the owner come up, an' did reäte
    Me as if I would car off his ground.
But his vield an' the grass wer-a-let,
    An' the damage that he could a-took
Wer at mwost that the while I did open the geäte
    I did rub roun' the eye on the hook.
But 'tís drevèn out, Thomas, an' hevèn out.
        Trample noo grounds,
Unless you be after the hounds.

Ah! the Squiër o' Culver-dell Hall
    Wer as diff'rent as light is vrom dark,
Wi' zome vo'k that, as evenèn did vall,
    Had a-broke drough long grass in his park;
Vor he went, wi' a smile, vor to meet
    Wi' the trespassers while they did pass,
An' he zaid, 'I do fear you'll catch cwold in your veet,
    You've a-walk'd drough so much o' my grass.'
His mild words, Thomas, cut em lik' swords, Thomas,
        Newly a-whet,
An' went vurder wi' them than a dret.

The Railroad

An' while I went 'ithin a traïn,
A-ridèn on athirt the plaïn,
A-cleärèn swifter than a hound,
On twin-laid rails, the zwimmèn ground;
I cast my eyes 'ithin a park,
Upon a woak wi' grey-white bark,
An' while I kept his head my mark,
The rest did wheel around en.

An' when in life our love do cling
The clwosest round zome single thing,
We then do vind that all the rest
Do wheel roun' that, vor vu'st an' best;
Zoo while our life do last, mid nought
But what is good an' feäir be sought,
In word or deed, or heart or thought,
An' all the rest wheel round it.

Seats

When starbright maïdens be to zit
    In silken frocks, that they do wear,
The room mid have, as 'tis but fit,
    A han'some seat vor vo'k so feäir;
But we, in zun-dried vield an' wood,
    Ha' seats as good's a goolden chair.

Vor here, 'ithin the woody drong,
    A ribbèd elem-stem do lie,
A-vell'd in Spring, an' stratch'd along
    A bed o' graegles up knee-high,
A sheädy seat to rest, an' let
    The burnèn het o' noon goo by.

Or if you'd look, wi' wider scope,
  Out where the gray-tree'd plaïn do spread,
The ash bezide the zunny slope,
  Do sheäde a cool-aïr'd deäisy bed,
An' grassy seat, wi' spreadèn eaves
  O' rus'lèn leaves, above your head.

An' there the traïn mid come in zight,
  Too vur to hear a-rollèn by,
A-breathèn quick, in heästy flight,
  His breath o' twile, avore the sky,
The while the waggon, wi' his lwoad,
  Do crawl the rwoad a-windèn nigh.

Or now theäse happy holiday
  Do let vo'k rest their weäry lim's,
An' lwoaded haÿ's a-hangèn gray,
  Above the waggon-wheels' dry rims,
The meäd ha' seats in weäles or pooks,
  By windèn brooks, wi' crumblèn brims.

Or if you'd gi'e your thoughtvul mind
  To yonder long-vorseäken hall,
Then teäke a stwonèn seat behind
  The ivy on the broken wall,
An' learn how e'thly wealth an' might
  Mid clim' their height, an' then mid vall.

Sound o' Water

I born in town! oh no, my dawn
O' life broke here beside theäse lawn;
Not where pent aïr do roll along,
In darkness drough the wall-bound drong,
An' never bring the goo-coo's zong,

Nor sweets o' blossoms in the hedge,
Or bendèn rush, or sheenèn zedge,
   Or sounds o' flowèn water.

The aïr that I've a-breath'd did sheäke
The draps o' raïn upon the breäke,
An' bear aloft the swingèn lark,
An' huffle roun' the elem's bark,
In boughy grove, an' woody park,
An' brought us down the dewy dells,
The high-wound zongs o' nightingeäles,
   An' sounds o' flowèn water.

An' when the zun, wi' vi'ry rim,
'S a-zinkèn low, an' wearèn dim,
Here I, a-most too tired to stand,
Do leäve my work that's under hand
In pathless wood or oben land,
To rest 'ithin my thatchèn oves,
Wi' ruslèn win's in leafy groves,
   An' sounds o' flowèn water.

Trees be Company

When zummer's burnèn het's a-shed
Upon the droopèn grasses head,
A-drevèn under sheädy leaves
The workvo'k in their snow-white sleeves.
We then mid yearn to clim' the height,
  Where thorns be white, above the vern;
An' aïr do turn the zunsheen's might
  To softer light too weak to burn—
    On woodless downs we mid be free,
    But lowland trees be company.

Though downs mid show a wider view
O' green a-reachèn into blue
Than roads a-windèn in the glen,
An' ringèn wi' the sounds o' men;
The thissle's crown o' red an' blue
  In Fall's cwold dew do wither brown,
An' larks come down 'ithin the lew,
    As storms do brew, an' skies do frown—
      An' though the down do let us free,
      The lowland trees be company.

Where birds do zing, below the zun,
In trees above the blue-smok'd tun,
An' sheädes o' stems do auverstratch
The mossy path 'ithin the hatch;
If leaves be bright up over head,
  When Maÿ do shed its glitt'rèn light;
Or, in the blight o' Fall, do spread
  A yollor bed avore our zight—
    Whatever season it mid be,
    The trees be always company.

When dusky night do nearly hide
The path along the hedge's zide,
An' dailight's hwomely sounds be still
But sounds o' water at the mill;
Then if noo feäce we long'd to greet
  Could come to meet our lwonesome treäce
Or if noo peäce o' weary veet,
  However fleet, could reach its pleäce—
    However lwonesome we mid be,
    The trees would still be company.

I know Who

Aye, aye, vull rathe the zun mus' rise
To meäke us tired o' zunny skies,
A-sheenèn on the whole day drough,
From mornèn's dawn till evenèn's dew.
When trees be brown an' meäds be green,
An' skies be blue, an' streams do sheen,
An' thin-edg'd clouds be snowy white
Above the bluest hills in zight;
But I can let the daylight goo,
When I've a-met wi'– I know who.

In Spring I met her by a bed
O' laurels higher than her head;
The while a rwose hung white between
Her blushes an' the laurel's green;
An' then in Fall, I went along
The row of elems in the drong,
An' heärd her zing bezide the cows,
By yollor leaves o' meäple boughs;
But Fall or Spring is feäir to view
When day do bring me—I know who.

An' when, wi' wint'r a-comèn roun',
The purple he'th's a-feädèn brown,
An' hangèn vern's a-sheäkèn dead,
Bezide the hill's besheäded head:
An' black-wing'd rooks do glitter bright
Above my head, in peäler light;
Then though the birds do still the glee
That sounded in the zummer tree,
My heart is light the winter drough,
In me'th at night, wi'—I know who.

Jessie Lee

Above the timber's bendèn sh'ouds,
   The western wind did softly blow;
An' up avore the knap, the clouds
   Did ride as white as driven snow.
Vrom west to east the clouds did zwim
Wi' wind that plied the elem's lim';
Vrom west to east the stream did glide,
A-sheenèn wide, wi' windèn brim.

How feäir, I thought, avore the sky
   The slowly-zwimmèn clouds do look;
How soft the win's a-streamèn by;
   How bright do rool the weävy brook:
When there, a-passèn on my right,
A-walkèn slow, an' treadèn light,
Young Jessie Lee come by, an' there
Took all my ceäre, an' all my zight.

Vor lovely wer the looks her feäce
   Held up avore the western sky:
An' comely wer the steps her peäce
   Did meäke a-walkèn slowly by:
But I went east, wi' beätèn breast,
Wi' wind, an' cloud, an' brook, vor rest,
Wi' rest a-lost, vor Jessie gone
So lovely on, toward the west.

Blow on, O winds, athirt the hill;
   Zwim on, O clouds; O waters vall,
Down maeshy rocks, vrom mill to mill;
   I now can auverlook ye all.
But roll, O zun, an' bring to me
My day, if such a day there be,
When zome dear path to my abode
Shall be the road o' Jessie Lee.

True Love

As evenèn aïr, in green-treed Spring,
Do sheäke the new-sprung pa'sley bed,
An' wither'd ash-tree keys do swing
An' vall a-flutt'rèn roun' our head:
There, while the birds do zing their zong
In bushes down the ash-tree drong,
Come Jessie Lee, vor sweet's the pleäce
Your vaïce an' feäce can meäke vor me.

Below the buddèn ashes' height
We there can linger in the lew,
While boughs, a-gilded by the light,
Do sheen avore the sky o' blue:
But there by zettèn zun, or moon
A-risèn, time wull vlee too soon
Wi' Jessie Lee, vor sweet's the pleäce
Her vaïce an' feäce can meäke vor me.

Down where the darksome brook do flow,
Below the bridge's archèd wall,
Wi' alders dark, a-leanèn low,
Above the gloomy watervall;
There I've a-led ye hwome at night,
Wi' noo feäce else 'ithin my zight
But yours so feäir, an' sweet's the pleäce
Your vaïce an' feäce ha' meäde me there.

An' oh! when other years do come,
An' zettèn zuns, wi' yollor gleäre,
Drough western window-peänes, at hwome,
Do light upon my evenèn chair:

While day do weäne, an' dew do vall,
Be wi' me then, or else in call,
As time do vlee, vor sweet's the pleäce
Your vaïce an' feäce do meäke vor me.

Ah! you do smile, a-thinkèn light
O' my true words, but never mind;
Smile on, smile on, but still your flight
Would leäve me little jaÿ behind:
But let me not be zoo a-tried
Wi' you a-lost where I do bide,
O Jessie Lee, in any pleäce
Your vaïce an' feäce ha' blest vor me.

I'm sure that when a soul's a-brought
To this our life ov aïr an' land,
Woone mwore's a-mark'd in God's good thought,
To help, wi' love, his heart an' hand.
An' oh! if there should be in store
An angel here vor my poor door,
'Tis Jessie Lee, vor sweet's the pleäce
Her vaïce an' feäce can meäke vor me.

The Beän Vield

'Twer where the zun did warm the lewth,
An' win' did whiver in the sheäde,
The sweet-aïr'd beäns were out in blooth,
Down there 'ithin the elem gleäde;
A yollor-banded bee did come,
An' softly-pitch, wi' hushèn hum,
Upon a beän, an' there did sip,
Upon a swaÿèn blossom's lip:
An' there cried he, 'Aye, I can zee,
This blossom's all a-zent vor me.'

157

A-jilted up an' down, astride
Upon a lofty ho'se a-trot,
The meäster then come by wi' pride,
To zee the beäns that he'd a-got;
An' as he zot upon his ho'se,
The ho'se ageän did snort an' toss
His high-ear'd head, an' at the zight
Ov all the blossom, black an' white:
'Ah! ah!' thought he, the seäme's the bee,
'Theäse beäns be all a-zent vor me.'

Zoo let the worold's riches breed
A strife o' claïms, wi' weak and strong,
Vor now what cause have I to heed
Who's in the right, or in the wrong;
Since there do come drough yonder hatch,
An' bloom below the house's thatch,
The best o' maïdens, an' do own
That she is mine, an' mine alwone:
Zoo I can zee that love do gi'e
The best ov all good gifts to me.

Vor whose be all the crops an' land
A-won an' lost, an' bought, an zwold
Or whose, a-roll'd vrom hand to hand,
The highest money that's a-twold?
Vrom man to man a passèn on,
'Tis here to-day, to-morrow gone.
But there's a blessèn high above
It all—a soul o' stedvast love:
Zoo let it vlee, if God do gi'e
Sweet Jessie vor a gift to me.

The Wife a-Lost

Since I noo mwore do zee your feäce,
  Up steäirs or down below,
I'll zit me in the lwonesome pleäce,
  Where flat-bough'd beech do grow:
Below the beeches' bough, my love,
  Where you did never come,
An' I don't look to meet ye now,
  As I do look at hwome.

Since you noo mwore be at my zide,
  In walks in zummer het,
I'll goo alwone where mist do ride,
  Drough trees a-drippèn wet:
Below the raïn-wet bough, my love,
  Where you did never come,
An' I don't grieve to miss ye now,
  As I do grieve at home.

Since now bezide my dinner-bwoard
  Your vaïce do never sound,
I'll eat the bit I can avword,
  A-vield upon the ground;
Below the darksome bough, my love,
  Where you did never dine,
An' I don't grieve to miss ye now,
  As I at hwome do pine.

Since I do miss your vaïce an' feäce
  In praÿer at eventide,
I'll praÿ wi' woone sad vaïce vor greäce
  To goo where you do bide;
Above the tree an' bough, my love,
  Where you be gone avore,
An' be a-waïtèn vor me now,
  To come vor evermwore.

159

Out at Plough

Though cool avore the sheenèn sky
Do vall the sheädes below the copse,
The timber-trees, a-reachèn high,
Ha' zunsheen on their lofty tops,
Where yonder land's a-lyèn plow'd,
An' red, below the snow-white cloud,
An' vlocks o' pitchèn rooks do vwold
Their wings to walk upon the mwold,
    While floods be low,
      An' buds do grow,
        An' aïr do blow, a-broad, O.

But though the aïr is cwold below
The creakèn copses' darksome screen,
The truest sheäde do only show
How strong the warmer zun do sheen;
An' even times o' grief an' païn,
Ha' good a-comèn in their traïn,
An' 'tis but happiness do mark
The sheädes o' sorrow out so dark.
    As twile be sad,
      Or smiles be glad,
        Or times be bad, at hwome, O.

An' there the zunny land do lie
Below the hangèn, in the lew,
Wi' vurrows now a-crumblèn dry,
Below the plowman's dousty shoe;
An' there the bwoy do whissel sh'ill,
Below the skylark's merry bill,
Where primrwose beds do deck the zides
O' banks below the meäple wrides.
    As trees be bright
      Wi' bees in flight,
        An' weather's bright, abroad, O.

An' there, as sheenèn wheels do spin
Vull speed along the dousty rwoad,
He can but stan', an' wish 'ithin
His mind to be their happy lwoad,
That he mid gaïly ride, an' goo
To towns the rwoad mid teäke en drough,
An' zee, for woonce, the zights behind
The bluest hills his eyes can vind,
        O' towns, an' tow'rs,
        An' downs, an' flow'rs,
            In zunny hours, abroad, O.

But still, vor all the weather's feäir,
Below a cloudless sky o' blue,
The bwoy at plough do little ceäre
How vast the brightest day mid goo;
Vor he'd be glad to zee the zun
A-zettèn, wi' his work a-done,
That he, at hwome, mid still injaÿ
His happy bit ov evenèn plaÿ,
        So light's a lark
        Till night is dark,
            While dogs do bark, at hwome, O.

The Turn o' the Days

O the wings o' the rook wer a-glitterèn bright,
As he wheel'd on above, in the zun's evenèn light,
An' noo snow wer a-left, but in patches o' white,
    On the hill at the turn o' the days.
An' along on the slope wer the beäre-timber'd copse,
Wi' the dry wood a-sheäkèn, wi' red-twiggèd tops.
Vor the dry-flowèn wind, had a-blow'd off the drops
    O' the raïn, at the turn o' the days.

There the stream did run on, in the sheäde o' the hill,
So smooth in his flowèn, as if he stood still,
An' bright wi' the skylight, did slide to the mill,
  By the meäds, at the turn o' the days.
An' up by the copse, down along the hill brow,
Wer vurrows a-cut down, by men out at plough,
So straïght as the zunbeams, a-shot drough the bough
  O' the tree at the turn o' the days.

Then the boomèn wold clock in the tower did mark
His vive hours, avore the cool evenèn wer dark,
An' ivy did glitter a-clung round the bark
  O' the tree, at the turn o' the days.
An' womèn a-fraïd o' the road in the night,
Wer a-heästenèn on to reach hwome by the light,
A-castèn long sheädes on the road, a-dried white,
  Down the hill, at the turn o' the days.

The father an' mother did walk out to view
The moss-bedded snow-drop, a-sprung in the lew,
An' hear if the birds wer a-zingèn anew,
  In the boughs, at the turn o' the days.
An' young vo'k a-laughèn wi' smooth glossy feäce,
Did hie over vields, wi' a light-vooted peäce,
To friends where the tow'r did betoken a pleäce
  Among trees, at the turn o' the days.

My Love's Guardian Angel

As in the cool-aïr'd road I come by,
                    —in the night,
Under the moon-clim'd height o' the sky,
                    —in the night,
There by the lime's broad lim's as I did staÿ,
While in the aïr dark sheädes wer' at plaÿ

Up on the windor-glass that did keep
Lew vrom the wind, my true love asleep,
$\qquad$ —in the night.

While in the grey-wall'd height o' the tow'r,
$\qquad$ —in the night,
Sounded the midnight bell wi' the hour,
$\qquad$ —in the night,
There come a bright-heäir'd angel that shed
Light vrom her white robe's zilvery thread,
Wi' her vore-vinger held up to meäke
Silence around lest sleepers mid weäke,
$\qquad$ —in the night.
'Oh! then,' I whisper'd, 'do I behold
$\qquad$ —in the night.
Linda, my true-love, here in the cwold,
$\qquad$ —in the night?'
'No,' she meäde answer, 'you do misteäke:
She is asleep, 'tis I be aweäke;
I be her angel brightly a-drest,
Watchèn her slumber while she do rest,
$\qquad$ —in the night.'

'Zee how the clear win's, brisk in the bough,
$\qquad$ —in the night,
While they do pass, don't smite on her brow,
$\qquad$ —in the night;
Zee how the cloud-sheädes naïseless do zweep
Over the house-top where she's asleep.
You, too, goo on, though times mid be near,
When you, wi' me, mid speäk to her ear
$\qquad$ —in the night.'

Leeburn Mill

Ov all the meäds wi' shoals an' pools,
Where streams did sheäke the limber zedge,
An' milkèn vo'k did teäke their stools,
In evenèn zun-light under hedge:
Ov all the wears the brook did vill,
Or all the hatches where a sheet
O' foam did leäp below woone's veet,
The pleäce vor me wer Leeburn Mill.

An' while below the mossy wheel
All day the foamèn stream did roar,
An' up in mill the floatèn meal
Did pitch upon the sheäkèn vloor.
We then could vind but vew han's still,
Or veet a-restèn off the ground,
An' seldom hear the merry sound
O' geämes a-plaÿ'd at Leeburn Mill.

But when they let the stream goo free,
Bezide the drippèn wheel at rest,
An' leaves upon the poplar-tree
Wer dark avore the glowèn west;
An' when the clock, a-ringèn sh'ill,
Did slowly beät zome evenèn hour,
Oh! then 'ithin the leafy bow'r
Our tongues did run at Leeburn Mill.

An' when November's win' did blow,
Wi' hufflèn storms along the plain,
An' blacken'd leaves did lie below
The neäked tree, a-zoak'd wi' raïn,
I werden at a loss to vill
The darkest hour o' raïny skies,
If I did vind avore my eyes
The feäces down at Leeburn Mill.

164

FROM
POEMS OF RURAL LIFE
IN THE DORSET DIALECT
THIRD COLLECTION
1862

"Δωρίσδεν δ'ἔξεστι, δοκῶ, τοῖς Δωριέεσσι"

THEOCRITUS.

The Echo

About the tow'r an' churchyard wall,
  Out nearly overright our door,
A tongue ov wind did always call
  Whatever we did call avore.
The vaïce did mock our neämes, our cheers,
  Our merry laughs, our hands' loud claps,
An' mother's call 'Come, come, my dears'
                              —*my dears;*
  Or 'Do as I do bid, bad chaps'
                              —*bad chaps.*

An' when o' Zundays on the green,
  In frocks an' cwoats as gaÿ as new,
We walk'd wi' shoes a-meäde to sheen
  So black an' bright's a vull-ripe slooe
We then did hear the tongue ov aïr
  A-mockèn mother's vaïce so thin,
'Come, now the bell do goo vor praÿ'r'
                              —*vor pray'r;*
''Tis time to goo to church; come in'
                              —*come in.*

The night when little Anne, that died,
  Begun to zickèn, back in Maÿ,
An' she, at dusk ov evenèn-tide,
  Wer out wi' others at their plaÿ,
Within the churchyard that do keep
  Her little bed, the vaïce o' thin
Dark aïr, mock'd mother's call 'To sleep'
                              —*to sleep;*
''Tis bed time now, my love, come in'
                              —*come in.*

167

An' when our Jeäne come out so smart
   A-married, an' we help'd her in
To Henry's newly-païnted cart,
   The while the wheels begun to spin,
An' her gaÿ nods, vor all she smil'd,
   Did sheäke a tear-drop vrom each eye,
The vaïce mock'd mother's call, 'Dear child'
               —dear child;
'God bless ye evermwore; good bye'
               —good bye.

Naïghbour Plaÿmeätes

O jaÿ betide the dear wold mill,
   My naïghbour plaÿmeätes' happy hwome,
Wi' rollèn wheel, an' leäpèn foam,
   Below the overhangèn hill,
      Where, wide an' slow,
      The stream did flow,
An' flags did grow, an' lightly vlee
Below the grey-leav'd withy tree,
While clack, clack, clack, vrom hour to hour,
Wi' whirlèn stwone, an' streamèn flour,
Did goo the mill by cloty Stour.

An' there in geämes by evenèn skies,
   When Meäry zot her down to rest,
The broach upon her pankèn breast,
   Did quickly vall an' lightly rise,
      While swans did zwim
      In high-neck'd trim.
An' swallows skim the water, bright
Wi' whirlèn froth, in western light;
An' clack, clack, clack, that happy hour,
Wi' whirlèn stwone, an' streamèn flour,
Did goo the mill by cloty Stour.

Now mortery jeints, in streaks o' white,
   Along the geärdèn wall do show
In Maÿ, an' cherry boughs do blow,
   Wi' bloomèn tutties, snowy white,
      Where rollèn round,
      Wi' rumblèn sound,
The wheel woonce drown'd the vaïce so dear
To me. I faïn would goo to hear
The clack, clack, clack, vor woone short hour,
Wi' whirlèn stwone, an' streamèn flour,
Bezide the mill on cloty Stour.

But should I vind a-heavèn now
   Her breast wi' aïr o' thik dear pleäce?
Or zee dark locks by such a brow,
   Or het o' plaÿ on such a feäce?
      No! She's now staïd,
      An' where she plaÿ'd,
There's noo such maïd that now ha' took
The pleäce that she ha' long vorsook,
Though clack, clack, clack, vrom hour to hour,
Wi' whirlèn stwone an' streamèn flour,
Do goo the mill by cloty Stour.

An' still the pulley rwope do heist
   The wheat vrom red-wheeled waggon beds.
An' ho'ses there wi' lwoads of grist,
   Do stand an' toss their heavy heads;
      But on the vloor,
      Or at the door,
Do show noo mwore the kindly feäce
Her father show'd about the pleäce,
As clack, clack, clack, vrom hour to hour,
Wi' whirlèn stwone, an' streamèn flour,
Did goo his mill by cloty Stour.

The Two Churches

A happy day, a happy year,
A zummer Zunday, dazzlèn clear,
I went athirt vrom Lea to Noke.
To goo to church wi' Fanny's vo'k:
The sky o' blue did only show
A cloud or two, so white as snow,
An' aïr did swaÿ, wi' softest strokes,
The eltrot roun' the dark-bough'd woaks.
O day o' rest when bells do toll!
O day a-blest to ev'ry soul!
How sweet the zwells o' Zunday bells.

An' on the cowslip-knap at Creech,
Below the grove o' steätely beech,
I heärd two tow'rs a-cheemèn clear,
Vrom woone I went, to woone drew near,
As they did call, by flow'ry ground,
The bright-shod veet vrom housen round,
A-drownèn wi' their holy call,
The goocoo an' the water-vall.
Die off, O bells o' my dear pleäce,
Ring out, O bells avore my feäce,
Vull sweet your zwells, O ding-dong bells.

Ah! then vor things that time did bring
My kinsvo'k, *Lea* had bells to ring;
An' then, ageän, vor what bevell
My wife's, why *Noke* church had a bell;
But soon wi' hopevul lives a-bound
In woone, we had woone tower's sound,
Vor our high jaÿs all vive bells rung,
Our losses had woone iron tongue.
Oh! ring all round, an' never mwoän

170

So deep an' slow woone bell alwone,
Vor sweet your swells o' vive clear bells.

Woak Hill

When sycamore leaves wer a-spreadèn,
      Green-ruddy, in hedges,
Bezide the red doust o' the ridges,
      A-dried at Woak Hill;

I packed up my goods all a-sheenèn
      Wi' long years o' handlèn,
On dousty red wheels ov a waggon,
      To ride at Woak Hill.

The brown thatchen ruf o' the dwellèn,
      I then wer a-leävèn,
Had shelter'd the sleek head o' Meäry,
      My bride at Woak Hill.

But now vor zome years, her light voot-vall
      'S a-lost vrom the vloorèn.
Too soon vor my jaÿ an' my childern,
      She died at Woak Hill.

But still I do think that, in soul,
      She do hover about us;
To ho vor her motherless childern,
      Her pride at Woak Hill.

Zoo—lest she should tell me hereafter
      I stole off 'ithout her,
An' left her, uncall'd at house-riddèn,
      To bide at Woak Hill—

I call'd her so fondly, wi' lippèns
  All soundless to others,
An' took her wi' aïr-reachèn hand,
  To my zide at Woak Hill.

On the road I did look round, a-talkèn
  To light at my shoulder,
An' then led her in at the door-way,
  Miles wide vrom Woak Hill.

An' that's why vo'k thought, vor a season,
  My mind wer a-wandrèn
Wi' sorrow, when I wer so sorely
  A-tried at Woak Hill.

But no; that my Meäry mid never
  Behold herzelf slighted,
I wanted to think that I guided
  My guide vrom Woak Hill.

The Hedger

Upon the hedge theäse bank did bear,
  Wi' lowonesome thought untwold in words,
I woonce did work, wi' noo sound there
  But my own strokes, an' chirpèn birds;
As down the west the zun went wan,
An' days brought on our Zunday's rest,
When sounds o' cheemèn bells did vill
The aïr, an' hook an' axe wer stïll.

Along the wold town-path vo'k went,
  An' met unknown, or friend wi' friend,
The maïd her busy mother zent,
  The mother wi' noo maïd to zend;

172

An' in the light the gleäzier's glass,
As he did pass, wer dazzlèn bright,
Or woone went by wi' down-cast head,
A-wrapp'd in blackness vor the dead.

An' then the bank, wi' risèn back,
   That's now a-most a-troddèn down,
Bore thorns wi' rind o' sheeny black,
   An' meäple stems o' ribby brown;
An' in the lewth o' theäse tree heads,
Wer primrwose beds a-sprung in blooth,
An' here a geäte, a-slammèn to,
Did let the slow-wheel'd plough roll drough.

Ov all that then went by, but vew
   Be now a-left behine', to beät
The mornèn flow'rs or evenèn dew,
   Or slam the woakèn vive-bar'd geäte;
But woone, my wife, so litty-stepp'd,
That have a-kept my path o' life,
Wi' her vew errands on the road,
Where woonce she bore her mother's lwoad.

In the Spring

My love is the maïd ov all maïdens,
   Though all mid be comely,
Her skin's lik' the jessamy blossom
   A-spread in the Spring.

Her smile is so sweet as a beäby's
   Young smile on his mother,
Her eyes be as bright as the dew drop
   A-shed in the Spring.

O grey-leafy pinks o' the geärden,
  Now bear her sweet blossoms;
Now deck wi' a rwose-bud, O briar,
  Her head in the Spring.

O light-rollèn wind blow me hither,
  The väice ov her talkèn,
Or bring vrom her veet the light doust,
  She do tread in the Spring.

O zun, meäke the gil'cups all glitter,
  In goold all around her;
An' meäke o' the deäisys' white flowers
  A bed in the Spring.

O whissle, gäy birds, up bezide her,
  In drong-waÿ, an' woodlands,
O zing, swingèn lark, now the clouds,
  Be a-vled in the Spring.

An' who, you mid ax, be my praïses
  A-meäkèn so much o',
An' oh! 'tis the maïd I'm a-hopèn
  To wed in the Spring.

The Flood in the Spring

Last night below the elem in the lew
    Bright the sky did gleam
On water blue, while aïr did softly blow
    On the flowèn stream,
An' there wer gil'cups' buds untwold,
An' deäisies that begun to vwold
Their low-stemm'd blossoms vrom my zight
Ageän the night, an' evenèn's cwold.

174

But, oh! so cwold below the darksome cloud
 Soon the night-wind roar'd,
Wi' raïny storms that zent the zwollèn streams
 Over ev'ry vword.
The while the drippèn tow'r did tell
The hour, wi' storm-be-smother'd bell,
An' over ev'ry flower's bud
Roll'd on the flood, 'ithin the dell.

But when the zun arose, an' lik' a rwose
 Shone the mornèn sky;
An' roun' the woak, the wind a-blowèn weak,
 Softly whiver'd by.
Though drown'd wer still the deaïsy bed
Below the flood, its feäce instead
O' flow'ry grown', below our shoes
Show'd feäirest views o' skies o'er head.

An' zoo to try if all our faïth is true
 Jaÿ mid end in tears,
An' hope, woonce feäir, mid saddèn into fear,
 Here in e'thly years.
But He that tried our soul do know
To meäke us good amends, an' show
Instead o' things a-took awaÿ,
Some higher jaÿ that He'll bestow.

Comen Hwome

As clouds did ride wi' heästy flight,
An' woods did swaÿ upon the height,
An' bleädes o' grass did sheäke, below
The hedge-row bramble's swingèn bow,
I come back hwome where winds did zwell,
 In whirls along the woody gleädes,
 On primrwose beds, in windy sheädes,
To Burnley's dark-tree'd dell.

There hills do screen the timber's bough,
The trees do screen the leäze's brow,
The timber-sheäded leäze do bear
A beäten path that we do wear.
The path do stripe the leäze's zide,
    To willows at the river's edge.
    Where hufflèn winds did sheäke the zedge,
An' sparklèn weäves did glide.

An' where the river, bend by bend,
Do dräin our meäd, an' mark its end,
The hangèn leäze do teäke our cows,
    An' trees do sheäde em wi' their boughs,
An' I the quicker beät the road,
    To zee a-comèn into view,
    Still greener vrom the sky-line's blue,
Wold Burnley our abode.

The Rwose in the Dark

In zummer, leäte at evenèn tide,
    I zot to spend a moonless hour
'Ithin the window, wi' the zide
    A-bound wi' rwoses out in flow'r,
Bezide the bow'r, vorsook o' birds,
An' listen'd to my true-love's words.

A-risèn to her comely height,
    She push'd the swingèn ceäsement round;
And I could hear, beyond my zight,
    The win'-blow'd beech-tree softly sound,
On higher ground, a-swayèn slow,
On drough my happy hour below.

An' tho' the darkness then did hide
  The dewy rwose's blushèn bloom,
He still did cast sweet aïr inside
  To Jeäne, a-chattèn in the room;
An' though the gloom did hide her feäce,
Her words did bind me to the pleäce.

An' there, while she, wi' runnèn tongue,
  Did talk unseen 'ithin the hall,
I thought her like the rwose that flung
  His sweetness vrom his darken'd ball,
'Ithout the wall, an' sweet's the zight
Ov her bright feäce, by mornèn light.

Zummer Winds

Let me work, but mid noo tie
Hold me vrom the oben sky,
When zummer winds, in playsome flight,
Do blow on vields in noon-day light,
Or ruslèn trees, in twilight night.
      Sweet's a stroll,
By flow'ry knowl, or blue-feäcèd pool
That zummer win's do ruffle cool.

When the moon's broad light do vill
Plaïns, a-sheenèn down the hill;
A-glitterèn on window glass,
O then, while zummer win's do pass
The rippled brook, an' swayèn grass,
      Sweet's a walk,
Where we do talk, wi' feäces bright,
In whispers in the peacevul night.

When the swayèn men do mow
Flow'ry grass, wi' zweepèn blow,

177

In het a-most enough to dry
The flat-spread clote-leaf that do lie
Upon the stream a-stealèn by,
    Sweet's their rest,
Upon the breast o' knap or mound
Out where the goocoo's vaïce do sound.

Where the sleek-heäir'd maïd do zit
Out o' door to zew or knit,
Below the elem where the spring
'S a-runnèn, an' the road do bring
The people by to hear her zing,
    On the green,
Where she's a-zeen, an' she can zee,
O gaÿ is she below the tree.

Come, O zummer wind, an' bring
Sounds o' birds as they do zing,
An' bring the smell o' bloomèn maÿ,
An' bring the smell o' new-mow'd haÿ;
Come fan my feäce as I do straÿ,
    Fan the heäir
O' Jessie feäir; fan her cool,
By the weäves o' stream or pool.

The Neäme Letters

When high-flown larks wer on the wing,
A warm-aïr'd holiday in Spring.
We stroll'd, 'ithout a ceäre or frown,
    Up roun' the down at Meldonley;
An' where the hawthorn-tree did stand
Alwone, but still wi' mwore at hand,
We zot wi' sheädes o' clouds on high
    A-flittèn by, at Meldonley.

An' there, the while the tree did sheäde
Their gigglèn heads, my knife's keen bleäde
Carved out, in turf avore my knee,
   J. L., T. D., at Meldonley.
'Twer Jessie Lee J. L. did meän,
T. D. did stan' vor Thomas Deäne;
The 'L' I scratch'd but slight, vor he
   Mid soon be D, at Meldonley.

An' when the vields o' wheat did spread
Vrom hedge to hedge in sheets o' red
An' bennets wer a-sheäkèn brown,
   Upon the down at Meldonley,
We stroll'd ageän along the hill,
An' at the hawthorn-tree stood still,
To zee J. L. vor Jessie Lee,
   An' my T. D., at Meldonley.

The grey-poll'd bennet-stems did hem
Each half-hid letter's zunken rim,
By leädy's-vingers that did spread
   In yollow red, at Meldonley.
An' heärebells there wi' light blue bell
Shook soundless on the letter L,
To ment the bells when L vor Lee
   Become a D at Meldonley.

Vor Jessie, now my wife, do strive
Wi' me in life, an' we do thrive;
Two sleek-heäired meäres do sprackly pull
   My waggon vull, at Meldonley;
An' small-hoof'd sheep, in vleeces white
Wi' quickly-pankèn zides, do bite
My thymy grass, a-mark'd vor me
   In black, T.D., at Meldonley.

The New House a-gettèn Wold

Ah! when our wedded life begun,
　　Theäse clean-wall'd house of ours wer new;
Wi' thatch as yollor as the zun
　　Avore the cloudless sky o' blue;
The sky o' blue that then did bound
The blue-hilled worold's flow'ry ground.

An' we've a-vound it weather-brown'd,
　　As Spring-tide blossoms oben'd white,
Or Fall did shed, on zunburnt ground,
　　Red apples from their leafy height:
Their leafy height, that Winter soon
Left leafless to the cool-feäced moon.

An' raïn-bred moss ha' staïn'd wi' green
　　The smooth-feäced wall's white-morter'd streaks,
The while our childern zot between
　　Our seats avore the fleäme's red peaks:
The fleäme's red peaks, till axan white
Did quench em vor the long-sleep'd night.

The bloom that woonce did overspread
　　Your rounded cheäk, as time went by,
A-shrinkèn to a patch o' red,
　　Did feäde so soft's the evenèn sky:
The evenèn sky, my faithful wife,
O' days as feäir's our happy life.

Zummer Stream

Ah! then the grassy-meäded Maȳ
Did warm the passèn year, an' gleam
Upon the yollow-grounded stream,
That still by beech-tree sheädes do straȳ.
The light o' weäves, a-runnèn there,
    Did plaȳ on leaves up over head,
An' vishes sceäly zides did gleäre,
    A-dartèn on the shallow bed,
An' like the stream a-slidèn on,
My zun out-measur'd time's agone.

There by the path, in grass knee-high,
Wer buttervlees in giddy flight,
All white above the deäisies white,
Or blue below the deep blue sky.
Then glowèn warm wer ev'ry brow,
O' maïd, or man, in zummer het,
An' warm did glow the cheäks I met
That time, noo mwore to meet em now.
As brooks, a-slidèn on their bed,
My season-measur'd time's a-vled.

Vrom yonder window, in the thatch,
Did sound the maïdens' merry words,
As I did stand, by zingèn birds,
Bezide the elem-sheäded hatch.
'Tis good to come back to the pleäce,
    Back to the time, to goo noo mwore;
'Tis good to meet the younger feäce
    A-mentèn others here avore.
As streams do glide by green mead-grass,
My zummer-brighten'd years do pass.

Eclogue

Come and Zee us in the Zummer

John; William; William's Bwoy; and William's Maïd
at Feäir.

JOHN

Zoo here be your childern, a-sheärèn
Your feäir-day, an' each wi' a feäirèn.

WILLIAM

Aye, well, there's noo peace 'ithout comèn
To stannèn an' show, in the zummer.

JOHN

An' how is your Jeäne? still as merry
As ever, wi' cheäks lik' a cherry?

WILLIAM

Still merry, but beauty's as feädesome
'S the raïn's gowèn bow in the zummer.

JOHN

Well now, I do hope we shall vind ye
Come soon, wi' your childern behind ye,
To Stowe, while o' bwoth zides o' hedges,
The zunsheen do glow in the zummer.

WILLIAM

Well, aye, when the mowèn is over,
An' ee-grass o whiten wi' clover.
A man's a-tired out, vor much walken,
The while he do mow in the zummer.

WILLIAM'S BWOY

I'll goo, an' we'll zet up a wicket,
An' have a good innèns at cricket;
An' teäke a good plounce in the water,
Where clote-leaves do grow in the zummer.

WILLIAM'S MAID

I'll goo, an' we'll plaÿ 'Thread the needle'
Or 'Huntèn the slipper', or wheedle
Young Jemmy to fiddle, an' reely
So brisk to an' fro in the zummer.

JOHN

An' Jeäne. Mind you don't come 'ithout her,
My wife is a-thinkèn about her;
At our house she'll find she's as welcome
'S the rwose that do blow in the zummer.

Lindenore

At Lindenore upon the steep,
  Bezide the trees a-reachèn high,
The while their lower limbs do zweep
  The river-stream a-flowèn by;
By greygle bells in beds o' blue,
Below the tree-stems in the lew,
Calm aïr do vind the rwose-bound door,
Ov Ellen Dare o' Lindenore.

An' there noo foam do hiss avore
  Swift bwoats, wi' water-plowèn keels,
An' there noo broad high-road's a-wore
  By vur-brought trav'lers' cracklèn wheels;
Noo crowd's a-passèn to and fro,
Upon the bridge's high-sprung bow:
An' vew but I do seek the door
Ov Ellen Dare o' Lindenore.

Vor there the town, wi' zun-bright walls,
  Do sheen vur off, by hills o' grey,
An' town-vo'k ha' but seldom calls
  O' business there, from day to day:
But Ellen didden leäve her ruf
To be admir'd, an' that's enough—
Vor I've a-vound 'ithin her door,
Feäir Ellen Dare o' Lindenore.

Treat Well your Wife

No, no, good Meäster Collins cried,
Why you've a good wife at your zide;
Zoo do believe the heart is true
That gi'ed up all bezide vor you,
An' still beheäve as you begun
To seek the love that you've a-won
    When woonce in dewy June,
In hours o' hope soft eyes did flash,
Each bright below his sheädy lash,
    A-glisnèn to the moon.

Think how her girlhood met noo ceäre
To peäle the bloom her feäce did weär,
An' how her glossy temple prest
Her pillow down, in still-feäced rest,
While sheädes o' window bars did vall
In moonlight on the gloomy wall,
    In cool-aïr'd nights o' June;
The while her lids, wi' bendèn streäks
O' lashes, met above her cheäks,
    A-bloomèn to the moon.

Think how she left her childhood's pleäce,
An' only sister's long-known feäce,

184

An' brother's jokes so much a-miss'd,
An' mother's cheäk, the last a-kiss'd;
An' how she lighted down avore
Her new abode, a husband's door,
    Your weddèn night in June;
Wi' heart that beät wi' hope an' fear,
While on each eye-lash hung a tear,
    A-glisnèn to the moon.

Think how her father zot all dum',
A-thinkèn on her, back at hwome,
The while grey axan gather'd thick,
On dyèn embers, on the brick;
An' how her mother look'd abroad,
Drough window, down the moon-bright road,
    Thik cloudless night o' June,
Wi' tears upon her lashes big
As raïn-drops on a slender twig,
    A-glisnèn to the moon.

Zoo don't zit thoughtless at your cup
An' keep your wife a-waïtèn up,
The while the clock's a-tickèn slow
The chilly hours o' vrost an' snow,
Until the zinkèn candle's light
Is out avore her drowsy sight,
    A-dimm'd wi' grief too soon;
A-leäven there alwone to murn
The feädèn cheäk that woonce did burn,
    A-bloomèn to the moon.

Hawthorn Down

All up the down's cool brow
    I work'd in noontide's gleäre,
On where the slow-wheel'd plow
    'D a-wore the grass half bare.

185

An' gil'cups quiver'd quick,
  As aïr did pass,
An' deäisies huddled thick
  Among the grass.

The while my eärms did swing
  Wi' work I had on hand,
The quick-wing'd lark did zing
  Above the green-tree'd land,
An' bwoys below me chafed
  The dog vor fun,
An' he, vor all they laef'd,
  Did meäke em run.

The south zide o' the hill,
  My own tun-smoke rose blue,—
In North Coomb, near the mill,
  My mother's wer in view—
Where woonce her vier vor all
  Ov us did burn,
As I have childern small
Round mine in turn.

An' zoo I still wull cheer
  Her life wi' my small store,
As she do drop a tear
  Bezide her lwonesome door.
The love that I do owe
  Her ruf, I'll paÿ,
An' then zit down below
  My own wi' jaÿ.

Oben Vields

Well, you mid keep the town an' street,
Wi' grassless stwones to beät your veet,
An' zunless windows where your brows
Be never cooled by swaÿèn boughs;
An' let me end, as I begun,
My days in oben aïr an' zun,
Where zummer win's a-blowèn sweet,
Wi' blooth o' trees as white's a sheet;
Or swaÿèn boughs, a-bendèn low
Wi' rip'nèn apples in a row,
An' we a-risèn rathe do meet
The bright'nèn dawn wi' dewy veet,
An' leäve, at night, the vootless groves,
To rest 'ithin our thatchen oves.
An' here our childern still do bruise
The deäisy buds wi' tiny shoes,
As we did meet avore em, free
Vrom ceäre, in plaÿ below the tree.
An' there in me'th their lively eyes
Do glissen to the zunny skies,
As aïr do blow, wi' leäzy peäce
To cool, in sheäde, their burnèn feäce.
Where leaves o' spreadèn docks do hide
The zawpit's timber-lwoaded zide,
An' trees do lie, wi' scraggy limbs,
Among the deäisy's crimson rims.
An' they, so proud, wi' eärms a-spread
To keep their balance good, do tread
Wi' ceäreful steps o' tiny zoles
The narrow zides o' trees an' poles.
An' zoo I'll leäve vor your light veet
The peävement o' the zunless strect,
While I do end, as I begun,
My days in oben aïr an' zun.

Times o' Year

Here did swaÿ the eltrot flow'rs,
When the hours o' night wer vew,
An' the zun, wi' eärly beams
Brighten'd streams, an' dried the dew,
An' the goocoo there did greet
Passers by wi' dousty veet.

There the milkmaïd hung her brow
By the cow, a-sheenèn red;
An' the dog, wi' upward looks,
Watch'd the rooks above his head,
An' the brook, vrom bow to bow,
Here went swift, an' there wer slow.

Now the cwolder-blowèn blast,
Here do cast vrom elems' heads
Feäded leaves, a-whirlèn round,
Down to ground, in yollow beds,
Ruslèn under milkers' shoes,
When the day do dry the dews.

Soon shall grass, a-vrosted bright,
Glisten white instead o' green,
An' the wind shall smite the cows,
Where the boughs be now their screen.
Things do change as years do vlee;
What ha' years in store vor me?

To Me

At night, as drough the meäd I took my waÿ,
In aïr a-sweeten'd by the new-meäde haÿ,
A stream a-vallèn down a rock did sound,
Though out o' zight wer foam an' stwone to me.

Behind the knap, above the gloomy copse,
The wind did russle in the trees' high tops,
Though evenèn darkness, an' the risèn hill,
Kept all the quiv'rèn leaves unshown to me,

Within the copse, below the zunless sky,
I heärd a nightèngeäle, a-warblèn high
Her lwoansome zong, a-hidden vrom my zight,
An' showèn nothèn but her mwoan to me.

An' by a house, where ɪ woses hung avore
The thatch-brow'd window, an' the oben door,
I heärd the merry words, an' hearty laugh
O' zome feäir maid, as yet unknown to me.

High over head the white-rimm'd clouds went on,
Wi' woone a-comèn up, vor woone a-gone;
An' feäir they floated in their sky-back'd flight,
But still they never meäde a sound to me.

An' there the miller, down the stream did float
Wi' all his childern, in his white-saïl'd bwoat,
Vur off, beyond the stragglèn cows in meäd,
But zent noo vaïce, athirt the ground, to me.

An' then a buttervlee, in zultry light,
A-wheelèn on about me, vier-bright,
Did show the gaÿest colors to my eye,
But still did bring noo vaïce around to me.

I met the merry laugher on the down,
Bezide her mother, on the path to town,
An' oh! her sheäpe wer comely to the zight,
But wordless then wer she a-vound to me.

Zoo, sweet ov unzeen things mid be sound,
An' feäir to zight mid soundless things be vound,
But I've the laugh to hear, an' feäce to zee,
Vor they be now my own, a-bound to me.

Tweil

The rick ov our last zummer's haulèn
   Now vrom grey's a-feäded dark,
An' off the barken raïl's a-vallèn,
   Day by day, the rottèn bark.—
But short's the time our works do stand,
So feäir's we put em out ov hand.
Vor time a-passèn, wet an' dry,
Do spweïl em wi' his changèn sky,
The while wi' strivèn hope, we men,
   Though a-ruèn time's undoèn,
Still do tweil an' tweil ageän.

In wall-zide sheädes, by leafy bowers,
   Underneath the swaÿèn tree,
O' leäte, as round the bloomèn flowers,
   Lowly humm'd the giddy bee,
My childern's small left voot did smite
Their tiny speäde, the while the right
Did trample on a deäisy head,
Bezïde the flower's dousty bed,
An' though their work wer idle then,
   They a-smilèn, an' a-tweilèn,
Still did work an' work ageän.

Now their little limbs be stronger,
   Deeper now their vaïce do sound;
An' their little veet be longer,
   An' do tread on other ground;
An' rust is on the little bleädes
   Ov all the broken-hafted speädes,
An' flow'rs that wer my hope an' pride
Ha' long agoo a-bloom'd an' died,
But still as I did leäbor then
   Vor love ov all them childern small,
Zoo now I'll tweil an' tweil ageän.

When the smokeless tun's a-growèn
   Cwold as dew below the stars,
An' when the vier noo mwore's a-glowèn
   Red between the window bars,
We then do laÿ our weary heads
In peace upon their nightly beds,
An' gi'e woone sock, wi' heavèn breast,
An' then breathe soft the breath o' rest,
Till day do call the sons o' men
   Vrom night-sleep's blackness, vull o' sprackness,
Out abroad to tweil ageän.

Where the vaïce o' the winds is mildest,
   In the plaïn, their stroke is keen;
Where their dreatnèn vaïce is wildest,
   In the grove, the grove's our screen.
An' where the worold in their strife
Do dreatèn mwost our tweilsome life,
Why there Almighty ceäre mid cast
A better screen ageän the blast.
Zoo I woon't live in fear o' men,
   But, man-neglected, God-directed,
Still wull tweil an' tweil ageän.

The Broken Heart

News o' grief had overteäken
Dark-ey'd Fanny, now vorseäken;
There she zot, wi' breast a-heavèn,
While vrom zide to zide, wi' grievèn,
Vell her head, wi' tears a-creepèn
Down her cheäks, in bitter weepèn.
There wer still the ribbon-bow
She tied avore her hour ov woe,

191

An' there wer still the han's that tied it
       Hangèn white,
       Or wringèn tight,
In ceäre that drown'd all ceäre bezide it.

When a man, wi' heartless slightèn,
Mid become a maïden's blightèn,
He mid ceärlessly vorseäke her,
But must answer to her Meäker;
He mid slight, wi' selfish blindness,
All her deeds o' lovèn-kindness,
God wull waïgh em wi' the slightèn
That mid be her love's requitèn;
He do look on each deceiver,
       He do know
       What weight o' woe
Do breäk the heart ov ev'ry griever.

Evenèn Light

The while I took my bit o' rest,
  Below my house's eastern sheäde,
  The things that stood in vield an' gleäde
Wer bright in zunsheen vrom the west.
    There bright wer east-ward mound an' wall,
    An' bright wer trees, arisèn tall,
An' bright did break 'ithin the brook,
  Down rocks, the watervall.

There deep 'ithin my pworches bow
  Did hang my heavy woaken door,
  An' in beyond en, on the vloor,
The evenèn dusk did gather slow;
    But bright did gleäre the twinklèn spwokes
    O' runnèn carriage wheels, as vo'ks
Out east did ride along the road,
  Bezide the low-bough'd woaks,

An' I'd a-lost the zun vrom view,
  Until ageän his feäce mid rise,
  A-sheenèn vrom the eastern skies
To brighten up the rwosc-borne dew;
    But still his lingrèn light did gi'e
    My heart a touchèn jaÿ, to zee
His beams a-shed, wi' stratchèn sheäde,
    On east-ward wall an' tree.

When jaÿ, a-zent me vrom above,
  Vrom my sad heart is now agone,
  An' others be a-walkèn on,
Amid the light ov Heavèn's love,
    Oh! then vor lovèn-kindness seäke,
    Mid I rejäice that zome do teäke
My hopes a-gone, until ageän
    My happy dawn do breäk.

The Wheel Routs

'Tis true I brought noo fortune hwome
  Wi' Jenny, vor her honeymoon,
But still a goodish hansel come
  Behind her perty soon,
Vor stick, an' dish, an' spoon, all vell
To Jeäne, vrom Aunt o' Camwy dell.

Zoo all the lot o' stuff a-tied
  Upon the plow, a tidy tod,
On gravel-crunchèn wheels did ride,
  Wi' ho'ses, iron-shod,
That, as their heads did nod, my whip
Did guide along wi' lightsome flip.

An' there it rod 'ithin the rwope,
  Astraïn'd athirt, an' straïn'd along,

Down Thornhay's evenèn-lighted slope
  An' up the beech-tree drong;
Where wheels a-bound so strong, cut out
On either zide a deep-zunk rout.

An' when at Fall the trees wer brown,
  Above the bennet-bearèn land,
When beech-leaves slowly whiver'd down,
  By evenèn winds a-fann'd;
The routs wer each a band o' red,
A-vill'd by drifted beech-leaves dead.

An' when, in Winter's leafless light,
  The keener eastern wind did blow,
An' scatter down, avore my zight,
  A chilly cwoat o' snow;
The routs ageän did show vull bright,
In two long streaks o' glitt'rèn white.

But when, upon our weddèn night,
  The cart's light wheels, a-rollèn round,
Brought Jenny hwome, they run too light
  To mark the yieldèn ground;
Or welcome would be vound a peäir
O' green-vill'd routs a-runnèn there.

Zoo let me never bring 'ithin
  My dwellèn what's a-won by wrong,
An' can't come in 'ithout a sin;
  Vor only zee how long
The waggon marks in drong, did show
Wi' leaves, wi' grass, wi' groun', wi' snow.

Lizzie

O Lizzie is so mild o' mind,
　　Vor ever kind, an' ever true;
A-smilèn, while her lids do rise
　　To show her eyes as bright as dew.
An' comely do she look at night,
A-dancèn in her skirt o' white,
An' blushèn wi' a rwose o' red
Bezide her glossy head.

Feäir is the rwose o' blushèn hue,
　　Behung wi' dew, in mornèn's hour,
Feäir is the rwose, so sweet below
　　The noontide glow, bezide the bow'r.
Vull feäir, an' eet I'd rather zee
The rwose a-gather'd off the tree,
An' bloomèn still with blossom red,
By Lizzie's glossy head.

Mid peace droughout her e'thly day,
　　Betide her waÿ, to happy rest,
An' mid she, all her weanèn life,
　　Or maïd or wife, be loved and blest.
Though I mid never zing anew
To neäme the maïd so feäir an' true,
A-blushèn, wi' a rwose o' red,
Bezíde her glossy head.

Blessens a-Left

Lik' souls a-toss'd at sea I bore
　　Sad strokes o' trial, shock by shock,
An' now, lik' souls a-cast ashore
　　To rest upon the beäten rock,

I still do seem to hear the sound
O' wcäves that drove me vrom my track,
An' zee my strugglèn hopes a-drown'd,
An' all my jaÿs afloated back.
By storms a-toss'd, I'll gi'e God praïse,
Wi' much a-lost I still ha' jaÿs.
My peace is rest, my faïth is hope,
An' freedom's my unbounded scope.

Vor faïth mid blunt the sting o' fear,
   An' peace the pangs ov ills a-vound,
An' freedom vlee vrom evils near,
   Wi' wings to vwold on other ground.
Wi' much a-lost, my loss is small,
Vor though ov e'thly goods bereft,
A thousand times well worth em all
Be they good blessèns now a-left.
What e'th do own, to e'th mid vall,
But what's my own my own I'll call,
My faïth, an' peäce, the gifts o' greäce,
An' freedom still to shift my pleäce.

When I've a-had a tree to screen
   My meal-rest vrom the high zunn'd-sky,
Or ivy-holdèn wall between
   My head an' win's a-rustlèn by,
I had noo call vor han's to bring
Their seäv'ry daïnties at my nod,
But stoop'd a-drinkèn vrom the spring,
An' took my meal, wi' thanks to God,
Wi' faïth to keep me free o' dread,
An' peäce to sleep wi' steadvast head,
An' freedom's hands, an' veet unbound
To woone man's work, or woone seäme ground.

196

Fall Time

The gather'd clouds, a-hangèn low,
   Do meäke the woody ridge look dim;
An' raïn-vill'd streams do brisker flow,
   Arisèn higher to their brim.
In the tree, vrom lim' to lim',
      Leaves do drop
Vrom the top, all slowly down,
Yollor, to the gloomy groun'.

The rick's a-tipp'd an' weather-brown'd,
   An' thatch'd wi' zedge a-dried an' dead;
An' orcha'd apples, red half round,
   Have all a-happer'd down, a-shed
Underneath the trees' wide head.
      Ladders long,
Rong by rong, to clim' the tall
Trees, be hung upon the wall.

The crumpled leaves be now a-shed
   In mornèn winds a-blowèn keen;
When they wer green the moss wer dead,
   Now they be dead the moss is green.
Low the evenèn zun do sheen
      By the boughs,
Where the cows do swing their tails
Over the merry milkers' païls.

The Zilver-Weed

The zilver-weed upon the green,
   Out where my sons an' daughters plaÿ'd,
Had never time to bloom between
   The litty steps o' bwoy an' maïd.

But rwose-trees down along the wall,
  That then wer all the maïden's ceäre,
An' all a-trimm'd an' traïn'd, did bear
  Their bloomèn buds vrom Spring to Fall.

But now the zilver leaves do show
  To zummer day their goolden crown,
Wi' noo swift shoe-zoles' litty blow,
  In merry plaÿ to beät em down.
An' where vor years zome busy hand
  Did traïn the rwoses wide an' high;
Now woone by woone the trees do die,
  An' vew of all the row do stand.

Zummer Thoughts in Winter Time

Well, aye, last evenèn, as I shook
My locks ov haÿ by Leecombe brook,
The yollow zun did weakly glance
Upon the winter meäd askance,
A-castèn out my narrow sheäde
Athirt the brook, an' on the meäd.
The while ageän my lwonesome ears
Did russle weatherbeäten spears,
Below the withy's leafless head
That overhung the river's bed;
I there did think o' days that dried
The new-mow'd grass o' zummer-tide,
When white-sleev'd mowers' whetted bleädes
Rung sh'ill along the green-bough'd gleädes,
An' maïdens gaÿ, wi' plaÿsome chaps,
A-zot wi' dinners in their laps,
Did talk wi' merry words that rung
Around the ring, vrom tongue to tongue;
An' welcome, when the leaves ha' died,
Be zummer thoughts in winter-tide.

198

I'm out o' Door

I'm out, when, in the winter's blast,
    The zun, a-runnèn lowly round,
Do mark the sheädes the hedge do cast
    At noon, in hoarvrost, on the ground.
I'm out when snow's a-lyèn white
    In keen-aïr'd vields that I do pass,
An' moonbeams, vrom above, do smite
    On ice an' sleeper's window-glass.
        I'm out o' door,
        When win' do zweep,
        By hangèn steep,
        Or hollow deep,
                At Lindenore.

O welcome is the lewth a-vound
    By rustlèn copse, or ivied bank,
Or by the haÿ-rick, weather-brown'd
    By barken-grass, a-springèn rank;
Or where the waggon, vrom the team
    A-freed, is well a-housed vrom wet,
An' on the dousty cart-house beam
    Do hang the cobweb's white-lin'd net.
        While storms do roar,
        An' win' do zweep,
        By hangèn steep,
        Or hollow deep,
                At Lindenore.

An' when a good day's work 's a-done
    An' I do rest, the while a squall
Do rumble in the hollow tun,
    An' ivy-stems do whip the wall.
Then in the house do sound about
    My ears, dear vaïces vull or thin,

A praÿen vor the souls vur out
  At sea, an' cry wi' bibb'ren chin—
      Oh! shut the door.
      What soul can sleep,
      Upon the deep,
      When storms do zweep
              At Lindenore.

A Snowy Night

'Twer at night, an' a keen win' did blow
  Vrom the east under peäle-twinklèn stars,
All a-zweepèn along the white snow;
  On the groun', on the trees, on the bars,
Vrom the hedge where the win' russled drough.
  There a light-russlèn snow-doust did vall;
An' noo pleäce wer a-vound that wer lew,
  But the shed, or the ivy-hung wall.

Then I knock'd at the wold passage door
  Wi' the win'-driven snow on my locks;
Till, a-comèn along the cwold vloor,
  There my Jenny soon answer'd my knocks.
Then the wind, by the door a-swung wide,
  Flung some snow in her clear-bloomèn feäce,
An' she blink'd wi' her head all a-zide,
  An' a-chucklèn, went back to her pleäce.

An' in there, as we zot roun' the brands,
  Though the talkers wer maïnly the men,
Bloomèn Jeäne, wi' her work in her hands,
  Did put in a good word now an' then.
An' when I took my leave, though so bleäk
  Wer the weather, she went to the door,
Wi' a smile, an' a blush on the cheäk
  That the snow had a-smitten avore.

The Year-Clock

We zot bezide the leäfy wall,
Upon the bench at evenfall,
While aunt led off our minds vrom ceäre
Wi' veäiry teäles, I can't tell where:
An' vound us woone among her stock
O' feäbles, o' the girt Year-clock.
His feäce wer blue's the zummer skies,
An' wide's the zight o' lookèn eyes,
For hands, a zun wi' glowèn feäce,
An' peäler moon wi' swifter peäce,
Did wheel by stars o' twinklèn light,
By bright-wall'd day, an' dark-treed night;
An' down upon the high-sky'd land,
A-reachèn wide, on either hand,
Wer hill an' dell wi' win'-swaÿ'd trees,
An' lights a-zweepèn over seas,
An' gleamèn cliffs, an' bright-wall'd tow'rs,
Wi' sheädes a-markèn on the hours;
An' as the feäce, a-rollèn round,
Brought comely sheäpes along the ground,
The Spring did come in winsome steäte
Below a glowèn raïnbow geäte;
An' fan wi' aïr a-blowèn weak,
Her glossy heäir, an' rwosy cheäk,
As she did shed vrom oben hand,
The leäpèn zeed on vurrow'd land;
The while the rook, wi' heästy flight,
A-floatèn in the glowèn light,
Did bear avore her glossy breast
A stick to build her lofty nest,
An' strong-lim'b Tweil, wi' steady hands,
Did guide along the vallow lands
The heavy zull, wi' bright-sheär'd beam,

Avore the weäry oxen team.
Wi' Spring a-gone there come behind
Sweet Zummer, jaÿ ov ev'ry mind,
Wi' feäce a-beamèn to beguile
Our weäry souls ov ev'ry tweil.
While birds did warble in the dell
In softest aïr o' sweetest smell;
An' she, so winsome-feäir did vwold
Her comely limbs in green an' goold,
An' wear a rwosy wreath, wi' studs
O' berries green, an' new-born buds,
A-fring'd in colours vier-bright,
Wi' sheäpes o' buttervlees in flight.
When Zummer went, the next ov all
Did come the sheäpe o' brown-feäc'd Fall,
A-smilèn in a comely gown
O' green, a-shot wi' yollow-brown,
A-border'd wi' a goolden stripe
O' fringe, a-meäde o' corn-ears ripe,
An' up ageän her comely zide,
Upon her rounded eärm, did ride
A perty basket, all a-twin'd
O' slender stems wi' leaves an' rind,
A-vill'd wi' fruit the trees did shed,
All ripe, in purple, goold, an' red;
An' busy Leäbor there did come
A-zingèn zongs ov harvest hwome,
An' red-ear'd dogs did briskly run
Roun' cheervul Leisure wi' his gun,
Or stan' an' mark, wi' stedvast zight,
The speckled pa'tridge rise in flight.
An' next ageän to mild-feäc'd Fall
Did come peäle Winter, last ov all,
A-bendèn down, in thoughtvul mood,
Her head 'ithin a snow-white hood
A-deck'd wi' icy-jewels, bright
An' cwold as twinklèn stars o' night;

An' there wer weary Leäbor, slack
O' veet to keep her vrozen track,
A-lookèn off, wi' wistful eyes,
To reefs o' smoke, that there did rise
A-meltèn to the peäle-feäc'd zun,
Above the houses' lofty tun.
An' there the girt Year-clock did goo
By day an' night, vor ever true,
Wi' mighty wheels a-rollèn round
'Ithout a beät, 'ithout a sound.

The Humstrum

Why woonce, at Chris'mas-tide, avore
The wold year wer a-reckon'd out,
The humstrums here did come about,
A-soundèn up at ev'ry door.
But now a bow do never screäpe
   A humstrum, any where all round,
An' zome can't tell a humstrum's sheäpe,
   An' never heärd his jinglèn sound.
As *ing-an-ing* did ring the string,
As *ang-an-ang* the wires did clang.

The strings a-tighten'd lik' to crack
Athirt the canister's tin zide,
Did reach, a glitt'rèn, zide by zide,
Above the humstrum's hollow back.
An' there the bwoy, wi' bended stick,
   A-strung wi' heäir, to meäke a bow,
Did dreve his elbow, light'nèn quick,
   Athirt the strings from high to low.
As *ing-an-ing* did ring the string,
As *ang-an-ang* the wires did clang.

The mother there did stan' an' hush
Her child, to hear the jinglèn sound,
The merry maïd, a-scrubbèn round
Her white-steäv'd païl, did stop her brush.
The mis'ess there, vor wold time's seäke,
    Had gifts to gi'e, and smiles to show,
An' meäster, too, did stan' an' sheäke
    His two broad zides, a-chucklèn low,
While *ing-an-ing* did ring the string,
While *ang-an-ang* the wires did clang.

The plaÿers' pockets wer a-strout,
Wi' wold brown pence, a-rottlèn in,
Their zwangèn bags did soon begin,
Wi' brocks an' scraps, to plim well out.
The childern all did run an' poke
    Their heads vrom hatch or door, an' shout
A-runnèn back to wolder wo'k.
    Why, here! the humstrums be about!
As *ing-an-ing* did ring the string,
As *ang-an-ang* the wires did clang.

Heedless o' my Love

Oh! I vu'st know'd o' my true love,
    As the bright moon up above,
Though her brightness wer my pleasure,
    She wer heedless o' my love.
Tho' twer all gaÿ to my eyes,
Where her feäir feäce did arise,
She noo mwore thought upon my thoughts,
    Than the high moon in the skies.

Oh! I vu'st heärd her a-zingèn,
    As a sweet bird on a tree,

Though her zingèn wer my pleasure,
   'Twer noo zong she zung to me.
Though her sweet vaïce that wer nigh,
Meäde my wild heart to beat high,
She noo mwore thought upon my thoughts,
   Than the birds would passers by.

Oh! I vu'st know'd her a-weepèn,
   As a raïn-dimm'd mornèn sky,
Though her teär-drops dimm'd her blushes,
   They wer noo drops I could dry.
Ev'ry bright tear that did roll,
Wer a keen païn to my soul,
But noo heärt's pang she did then veel,
   Wer vor my words to console.

But the wold times be a-vanish'd,
   An' my true love is my bride.
An' her kind heart have a-meäde her.
   As an angel at my zide;
I've her best smiles that mid plaÿ,
I've her me'th when she is gaÿ,
When her tear-drops be a-rollèn,
I can now wipe em awaÿ.

Don't Ceäre

At the feäst, I do mind very well, all the vo'ks
   Wer a-took in a happerèn show'r,
But we chaps took the maïdens, an' kept em wi' clokes
   Under shelter, all dry as mill flour;
An' to my lot vell Jeäne, that's my bride,
That did titter, a-hung at my zide;
Zaid her aunt, 'Why the vo'k 'ull talk finely o' you,'
An', cried she, 'I don't ceäre if they do.'

When the time o' the feäst wer ageän a-come round,
　An' the vo'k wer a-gather'd woonce mwore,
Why she guess'd if she went there, she'd soon be
　　a-vound
　An' a-took seäfely hwome to her door.
Zaid her mother, ''Tis sure to be wet'.
Zaid her cousin, ''T'll raïn by zunset'.
Zaid her aunt, 'Why the clouds there do look black an'
　　blue',
An' zaid she, 'I don't ceäre if they do'.

An' at last, when she own'd I mid meäke her my bride,
　Vor to help me, an' sheäre all my lot,
An' wi' faïthvulness keep all her life at my zide,
　Though my waÿ mid be happy or not,
Zaid her naïghbours, 'Why wedlock's a clog,
An' a wife's a-tied up lik' a dog'.
Zaid her aunt, 'You'll vind trials enough vor to rue',
An' zaid she, 'I don't ceäre if I do.'

Now she's married, an' still in the midst ov her tweils
　She's as happy's the daylight is long,
So do goo out abroad wi' her feäce vull o' smiles,
　An' do work in the house wi' a zong.
An', zays woone, 'She don't grieve, you can tell.'
Zays another, 'Why, don't she look well!'
Zays her aunt, 'Why the young vo'k do envy you two',
An', zays she, 'I don't ceäre if they do'.

Now vor me I can zing in my business abrode,
　Though the storm do beät down on my poll,
There's a wife-brighten'd vier at the end o' my road,
　An' her love vor the jaÿ o' my soul.
Out o' door I wi' rogues mid be tried;
Out o' door be brow-beäten wi' pride;
Men mid scowl out o' door, if my wife is but true—
Let em scowl, 'I don't ceäre if they do'.

Kindness

Good Meäster Collins heärd woone day
A man a-talkèn, that did zay
It woulden answer to be kind,
He thought, to vo'k o' grov'lèn mind,
Vor they would only teäke it wrong,
That you be weak an' they be strong.
'No,' cried the goodman, 'never mind,
Let vo'k be thankless,—you be kind;
Don't do your good for e'thly ends
At man's own call vor man's amends.
Though souls befriended should remaïn
As thankless as the sea vor raïn,
On them the good's a-lost 'tis true,
But never can be lost to you.
Look on the cool-feäced moon at night
Wi' light-vull ring, at utmost height,
A-castèn down, in gleamèn strokes,
His beams upon the dim-bough'd woaks,
To show the cliff a-risèn steep,
To show the stream a-vallèn deep,
To show where windèn roads do leäd,
An' prickly thorns do ward the meäd.
While sheädes o' boughs do flutter dark
Upon the woak-trees' moon-bright bark,
There in the lewth, below the hill,
The nightèngeäle, wi' ringèn bill,
Do zing among the soft-aïr'd groves,
While up below the house's oves
The maïd, a-lookèn vrom her room
Drough window, in her youthvul bloom,
Do listen, wi' white ears among
Her glossy heäirlocks, to the zong.
If, then, the while the moon do light
207

The lwonesome zinger o' the night,
His cwold-beam'd light do seem to show
The prowlèn owls the mouse below.
What then? Because an evil will,
Ov his sweet good, mid meäke zome ill,
Shall all his feäce be kept behind
The dark-brow'd hills to leäve us blind?'

Daniel Dwithen, the Wise Chap

Dan Dwithen wer the chap to show
His naïghbours mwore than they did know,
Vor he could zee, wi' half a thought,
What zome could hardly be a-taught;
   An' he had never any doubt
Whatever 'twer, but he did know't,
An' had a-reach'd the bottom o't,
   Or soon could meäke it out.

Wi' narrow feäce, an' nose so thin
That light a'most shone drough the skin,
As he did talk, wi' his red peäir
O' lips, an' his vull eyes did steäre,
   What nippy looks friend Daniel wore,
An' how he smile as he did bring
Such reasons vor to clear a thing,
   As dather'd vo'k the mwore!

When woonce there come along the road
At night, zome show-vo'k, wi' a lwoad
Ov half the wild outlandish things
That crawl'd, or went wi' veet, or wings;
   Their elephant, to stratch his knees,
Walk'd up the road-zide turf, an' left
His tracks a-zunk wi' all his heft
   As big's a vinny cheese.

An' zoo next mornèn zome vo'k vound
The girt round tracks upon the ground,
An' view'd em all wi' stedvast eyes,
An' wi' their vingers spann'd their size,
    An' took their depth below the brink:
An' whether they mid be the tracks
O' things wi' witches on their backs,
    Or what, they coulden think.

At last friend Dan come up, an' brought
His wit to help their dizzy thought,
An' lookèn on an' off the ea'th,
He cried, a-drawèn a vull breath,
    Why, I do know; what, can't ye zee 't?
I'll bet a shillèn 'twer a deer
Broke out o' park, an' sprung on here,
    Wi' quoits upon his veet.

Turnèn Things Off

Upzides wi' Polly! no, he'd vind
That Poll would soon leäve him behind.
To turn things off! oh! she's too quick
To be a-caught by ev'ry trick.
Woone day our Jimmy stole down steäirs
On merry Polly unaweäres,
The while her nimble tongue did run
A-tellèn, all alive wi' fun,
To sister Anne, how Simon Heäre
Did hanker after her at feäir.
'He left,' cried Polly ,'cousin Jeäne,
An' kept wi' us all down the leäne,
An' which way ever we did leäd
He vollow'd over hill an' meäd;
An' wi' his head o' shaggy heäir,
209

An' sleek brown cwoat that he do weäre,
An' collar that did reach so high
'S his two red ears, or perty nigh,
He swung his täil, wi' steps o' pride,
Back right an' left, vrom zide to zide,
A-walkèn on, wi' heavy strides
A half behind, an' half upzides.'
'Who's that?' cried Jimmy, all agog;
An' thought he had her now han'-pat,
'That's Simon Heäre,' but no, 'Who's that?'
Cried she at woonce, 'Why Uncle's dog,
Wi' what have you a-been misled
I wonder. Tell me what I zaid.'
Woone evenèn as she zot beside
The wall the ranglèn vine do hide,
A-prattlèn on, as she did zend
Her needle, at her vinger's end.
On drough the work she had in hand,
Zome bran-new thing that she'd a-plann'd,
Jim overheärd her talk ageän
O' Robin Hine, ov Ivy Leäne,
'Oh! no, what he!' she cried in scorn,
'I wouldèn gie a penny vor'n;
The best ov him's outzide in view;
His cwoat is gaÿ enough, 'tis true,
But then the wold vo'k didden bring
En up to know a single thing,
An' as vor zingèn,—what do seem
His zingèn's nothèn but a scream.'
'So ho!' cried Jim, 'Who's that, then, Meäry,
That you be now a-talkèn o'?'
He thought to catch her then, but, no,
Cried Polly, 'Oh! why Jeäne's caneäry,
Wi' what have you a-been misled,
I wonder. Tell me what I zaid.'

A Lot o' Maïdens a-runnèn the Vields[1]

'Come on. Be sprack, a-laggèn back.'
'Oh! be thére any cows to hook?'
'Lauk she's afraïd, a silly maïd,'
Cows? No, the cows be down by brook.
'Oh here then, oh! here is a lot.'
'A lot o' what? what is it? what?'
'Why blackberries, as thick
As ever they can stick.'
'I've dewberries, oh! twice
As good as they; so nice.'
'Look here. Theäse boughs be all but blue
Wi' snags.'
           'Oh! gi'e me down a vew.'
'Come here, oh! do but look.'
'What's that? what is it now?'
'Why nuts a-slippèn shell.'
'Hee! hee! pull down the bough.'
'I wish I had a crook.'
'There zome o'm be a-vell.'
(*One sings*)
           'I wish I was on Bimport Hill
I would zit down and cry my vill.'
'Hee! hee! there's Jenny zomewhere nigh,
A-zingèn that she'd like to cry.'
(*Jenny sings*)
           'I would zit down and cry my vill
Until my tears would dreve a mill.'
'Oh! here's an ugly crawlèn thing,
A sneäke.' 'A slooworm; he wont sting.'
'Hee! hee! how she did squal an' hop,
A-spinnèn roun' so quick's a top.'
'Look here, oh! quick, be quick.'

[1] The idea, though but little of the substance, of this poem, will be found in a little Italian poem called *Caccia*, written by Franco Sacchetti.

'What is it? what then? where?'
'A rabbit.' 'No, a heäre.'
'Ooh! ooh! the thorns do prick,'
'How he did scote along the ground
As if he wer avore a hound.'
'Now mind the thistles.' 'Hee, hee, hee,
Why they be knapweeds.'
'No.' 'They be.'
'I've zome'hat in my shoe.'
'Zit down, an' sheäke it out.'
'Oh! emmets, oh! ooh, ooh,
A-crawlèn about.'
'What bird is that, O harken, hush.
How sweetly he do zing.'
'A nightingeäle.' 'La! no, a drush.'
'Oh! here's a funny thing.'
'Oh! how the bull do hook,
An' bleäre, an' fling the dirt.'
'Oh! won't he come athirt?'
'No, he's beyond the brook.'
'O lauk! a hornet rose
Up clwose avore my nose.'
'Oh! what wer that so white
Rush'd out o' thik tree's top?'
'An owl.' 'How I did hop,
How I do sheäke wi' fright.'
'A musheroom.' 'O lau!
    A twoadstool! Pwoison! Augh.
'What's that, a mouse?'
                                'O no,
Teäke ceäre, why 'tis a shrow.'
'Be sure don't let en come
An' run athirt your shoe
He'll meäke your voot so numb
That you wont veel a tooe.'[1]

---

[1] The folklore is, that if a shrew-mouse run over a person's foot
it will lame him.

'Oh! what wer that so loud
A-rumblèn?' 'Why a clap
O' thunder. Here's a cloud
O' raïn. I veel a drap.'
'A thunderstorm. Do raïn.
Run hwome wi' might an' maïn.'
Hee! hee! oh! there's a drop
A-trickled down my back. Hee! hee!'
'My head's as wet's a mop.'
'Oh! thunder,' 'there's a crack. Oh! Oh!'
'Oh! I've a-got the stitch, Oh!'
'Oh! I've a-lost my shoe, Oh!'
'There's Fanny into ditch, Oh!'
'I'm wet all drough an' drough, Oh!'

Good Night

While down the meäds wound slow,
    Water vor green-wheel'd mills,
Over the streams bright bow,
    Win' come vrom dark-back'd hills.
Birds on the win' shot along down steep
Slopes wi' a swift-swung zweep.
Dim weän'd the red-streak'd west.
Lim'-weary souls 'Good-rest'.

Up on the plough'd hill brow,
    Still wer the zull's wheel'd beam,
Still wer the red-wheel'd plough,
    Free o' the strong limb'd team,
Still wer the shop that the smith meäde ring,
Dark where the sparks did spring;
Low shot the zun's last beams.
Lim'-weary souls 'Good dreams'.

Where I vrom dark bank-sheädes
   Turn'd up the west hill road,
Where all the green grass bleädes
   Under the zunlight glow'd.
Startled I met, as the zunbeams plaÿ'd
Light, wi' a zunsmote maïd,
Come vor my day's last zight.
Zun-brighten'd maïd 'Good night'.

Went Hwome

Upon the slope, the hedge did bound
The vield wi' blossom-whited zide,
An' charlock patches, yollow-dyed,
Did reach along the white-soil'd ground
An' vo'k, a-comèn up vrom meäd,
   Brought gil-cup meal upon the shoe;
Or went on where the road did leäd,
   Wi' smeechy doust from heel to tooe.
As noon did smite, wi' burnèn light,
The road so white, to Meldonley.

An' I did tramp the zun-dried ground,
By hedge-climb'd hills, a-spread wi' flow'rs,
An' watershootèn dells, an' tow'rs,
By elem-trees a-hemm'd all round,
To zee a vew wold friends, about
   Wold Meldon, where I still ha' zome,
That bid me speed as I come out,
   An' now ha' bid me welcome hwome,
As I did goo, while skies wer blue,
Vrom view to view, to Meldonley.

An' there wer timber'd knaps, that show'd
Cool sheädes, vor rest, on grassy ground,

214

An' thatch-brow'd windows, flower-bound,
Where I could wish wer my abode.
I pass'd the maïd avore the spring,
   An' shepherd by the thornèn tree;
An' heärd the merry dréver zing,
   But met noo kith or kin to me,
Till I come down, vrom Meldon's crown
To rufs o' brown, at Meldonley.

FROM

POEMS

IN THE DORSET DIALECT

BY THE LATE REV. W. BARNES

· 1906 ·

(mostly written in 1867: the dates, unless otherwise stated, are of publication in the *Dorset
County Chronicle*)

The Wind at the Door

As day did darken on the dewless grass
There still wi' nwone a-come by me,
To staÿ a-while at hwome by me;
Within the house, all dumb by me,
I zot me sad as the eventide did pass.

An' there a win'-blast shook the rattlèn door,
An' seemed, as win' did mwone without,
As if my Jeäne, alwone without,
A-stannèn on the stone without,
Wer there a-come wi' happiness oonce mwore.

I went to door; an' out vrom trees above
My head, upon the blast by me,
Sweet blossoms wer a-cast by me,
As if my love, a-past by me,
Did fling em down—a token ov her love.

'Sweet blossoms o' the tree where I do murn,'
I thought, 'if you did blow vor her,
Vor apples that should grow vor her,
A-vallèn down below vor her,
O then how happy I should zee you kern.'

But no. Too soon I voun' my charm abroke.
Noo comely soul in white like her—
Noo soul a-steppèn light like her—
An' nwone o' comely height like her—
Went by; but all my grief ageän awoke.

1867

Winter A-Comen

I'm glad we have wood in store awhile,
Avore all the ground's avroze awhile;
Vor soon we must shut the door awhile
Vrom wind that's a-whirlèn snow.

The zwallows have all a-hied away,
The flowers have now a-died away,
An' boughs, wi' their leaves, a-dried away,
In wind do goo to an' fro.

Your walks in the ash-tree droves be cwold,
Your banks in the elem groves be cwold,
Your bench by the house's oves be cwold
Where zummer did leätely glow.

Noo rwose is a-bloomèn red to-day,
Noo pink vor your breast or head to-day,
A-deckèn the geärden bed to-day,
Do linger a-noddèn low.

Noo mwore is the swingèn lark above,
An aïr a-clouded dark above
Do stifle the zun's last spark above,
Where little blue sky do show.

Zoo now gi'e your cheäks a bloom to-night,
Where vier do het the room to-night,
A'dreven away the gloom to-night,
While winterly wind do blow.

1867

Winter Weather

When elem stems do rise, in row,
Dark brown, vrom hangèns under snow,
An' woods do reach as black as night
By slopèn vields o' cleänest white;
The shooters by the snowy rick,
Where trees be high, an' wood is thick,
A-markèn tracks the geäme do prick,
Do like the winter weather.

Or where do spread the grey-blue sheet
Ov ice, vor skeäter's glidèn veet
That they do lift, vrom zide to zide,
Long yards, an' hit em down to slide;
Or sliders, one a-tott'rèn slack
Of limb, an' one upon his back,
An' one upright, do keep his track—
Ha' fun, in winter weather.

When we at night, in snow an' gloom,
Did seek some neighbour's lighted room,
Though snow did show noo path avore,
Towards the house, we vound the door;
An' there, as round the brands, did spread
The creepèn vire o' cherry red,
Our veet vrom snow, vrom wind our head,
Wer warm, in winter weather.

Wherever day mid give our road
By knaps, or hollows over-snow'd;
By windy gaps, or lewer nooks,
Or bridgèd ice, o' vrozen brooks;
Still mid we all, when night do come,
Know where we have a peacevul hwome,
An' glowèn vire vor vingers numb
Wi' cwold, in winter weather.

1868

221

Clouds

A-ridèn slow, at lofty height,
  Wer' clouds, a-blown along the sky,
O' purple blue, an' pink, an' white,
  In pack an' pile, a-reachèn high,
A-shiftèn off, as they did goo,
  Their sheäpes, from new, ageän to new

An' zome like rocks an' tow'rs o' stwone,
  Or hills or woods, a-reächèn wide;
An' zome like roads, wi' doust a-blown,
  A-glitt'rèn white up off their zide,
A-comèn bright, ageän to feäde
  In sheäpes a-meäde to be unmeäde.

Zoo things do come, but never stand,
  In life. It mid be smiles or tears,
A joy in hope, an' one in hand,
  Zome grounds o' grief, an' zome o' fears,
It mid be good or mid be ill,
  But never long a-standèn still.

1868

The Broken Jug

JENNY AND JOHN

JEN.   As if you coudden leäve the jug alwone!
        Now you've a-smack'd my jug,
        Now you've a-whack'd my jug,
        Now you've a-crack'd my jug
          Ageän the stwone.

222

JOHN.   Why he must be a-crack'd unknown to you,
             Zoo don't belie the stwone,
             He scarce went nigh the stwone:
             He just went by the stwone,
                 An' broke in two.

JEN.   He, crack'd avore! no, he wer sound enough,
             Vrom back to lip, wer sound,
             To stand or tip wer sound,
             To hold or dip wer sound,
                 Don't talk such stuff.

JOHN.   How high then do the price o'n reach?
             I'd buy zome mwore, so good;
             I'd buy a score, so good;
             I'd buy a store, so good,
                 At twopence each.

JEN.   Indeed! with stwonen jugs a-zwold so dear.
                     (*slaps him*)
             No, there's a tap, vor lies;
             An' there's a slap, vor lies,
             An' there's a rap, vor lies,
                 About your ear.

JOHN.   Oh! there be pretty hands! a little dear.

   1867

Green

Our zummer way to church did wind about
The cliff, where ivy on the ledge wer green.

Our zummer way to town did skirt the wood,
Where sheenèn leaves in tree an' hedge wer green.

223

Our zummer way to milkèn in the meäd,
Wer on by brook, where fluttrèn zedge wer green.

Our hwomeward ways did all run into one,
Where moss upon the roofstwones' edge were green.

1867

White an' Blue

My love is o' comely height, an' straïght,
An' comely in all her waÿs and gaït;
In feäce she do show the rwose's hue,
An' her lids on her eyes be white on blue.

When Elemley clubmen walk'd in Maÿ,
An' vo'k come in clusters, ev'ry waÿ,
As soon as the zun dried up the dew,
An' clouds in the sky wer white on blue,

She come by the down, wi' trippèn talk,
By deäsies, an' sheenèn banks o' chalk,
An' brooks, where the crowvoot flow'rs did strew
The sky-tinted water, white on blue.

She nodded her head, as plaÿ'd the band;
She dapp'd wi' her voot, as she did stand;
She danced in a reel, a-weärèn new
A skirt wi' a jacket, white wi' blue.

I singled her out vrom thin an' stout,
Vrom slender an' stout I chose her out;
An' what, in the evenèn, could I do,
But gi'e her my breast-knot, white an' blue?

Written 31st October 1867

The Little Hwomestead

Where the zun did glow warm vrom his height,
On the vo'k, at their work, in white sleeves;
An' the goold-banded bee wer in flight,
Wi' the birds that did flit by the leaves,
There my two little children did run,
An' did rile, and did roll, in their fun;
An' did clips, in their hands
   Stick or stwone vor their plaÿ;
In their hands, that had little a-grown;
Vor their plaÿ, wi' a stick or a stwone.

As the zun down his high zummer bow
To the west o' the orcha'd did vall,
He did leäve the brown bee-hives, in row,
In the sheäde o' the houses gray wall;
An' the flowers, a-sheenen in bloom,
Zome a-lighted, an' zome in the gloom,
To the cool o' the air,
   An' the damp o' the dew:
O' the air, vrom the apple-tree sheädes,
An' the dew, on the grasses' green bleädes.

An' there were my orcha'd a-tined
Wi' a hedge on the steep-zided bank,
Where the ivy did twine roun' the rind
O' the wood-stems, an' trees in high rank;
Vor to keep out the wide-lippèd cow;
An' the stiff-snowted pigs, that would plough
Up the nesh-bleäded grass,
   By the young apple-trees;
The grass a-grown up to good height,
By the trees, that wi' blooth wer all white.

O when is a father's good time,
That do paÿ for his tweil wi' mwost jaÿ?
Is it when he's a-spenden his prime
Vor his children, still young in their plaÿ,
Or when they've a-grown to their height,
An' a-gone vrom his heärèn an' zight,
Wi' their mother's woone voice
   A-left hwome at the door:
A voice that noo longer do zing,
At the door that mwore seldom do swing?

The Mother's Dream[1]

I'd a dream to-night
   As I vell asleep
Oh! the touchèn zight
   Still do meäke me weep,—
Ov my little bwoy
That's a-took away;
Aye, about my joy
   I wer not to keep.

As in heaven high
   I my child did seek,
There, in traïn, come by
   Children feäir an' meek;
Each in lilywhite,
Wi' a lamp alight
Each wer clear to zight,
   But noo words did speak.

Then a-lookèn sad
   Come my child in turn;
But the lamp he had
   Oh! he didden burn;

[1] The English version is printed on p. 231.

226

He, to clear my doubt,
Zaid, a-turn'd about,
Your tears put en out;
   Mother, never murn.

1867

The Geäte A-Vallèn To

In the zunsheen of our zummers
   Wi' the häytime now a-come,
How busy wer we out a-vield
   Wi' vew a-left at hwome,
When waggons rumbled out ov yard
   Red wheeled, wi' body blue,
And back behind 'em loudly slamm'd
   The geäte a-vallèn to.

Drough day sheen ov how many years
   The geäte ha' now a-swung,
Behind the veet o' vull-grown men
   And vootsteps of the young.
Drough years o' days it swung to us
   Behind each little shoe,
As we tripped lightly on avore
   The geäte a-vallèn to.

In evenèn time o' starry night
   How mother zot at hwome
And kept her bläzing vire bright
   Till father should ha' come,
And how she quicken'd up and smiled,
   And stirred her vire anew,
To hear the trampèn ho'ses' steps
   And geäte a-vallèn to.

There's moon-sheen now in nights o' Fall
    When leaves be brown vrom green,
When to the slammèn o' the geäte
    Our Jenny's ears be keen,
When the wold dog do wag his taïl,
    And Jeän could tell to who,
As he do come in drough the geäte,
    The geäte a-vallèn to.

And oft do come a saddened hour
    When there must goo away
One well-beloved to our heart's core.
    Vor long, perhaps for aye:
And oh! it is a touchèn thing
    The lovèn heart must rue
To hear behind his last farewel
    The geäte a-vallèn to.

Written 13*th October* 1885

228

The Mother's Dream[1]

I'd a dream to-night
As I fell asleep,
Oh! the touching sight
Makes me still to weep:
Of my little lad,
Gone to leave me sad,
Aye, the child I had,
But was not to keep.

As in heaven high,
I my child did seek,
There, in train, came by
Children fair and meek,
Each in lily white,
With a lamp alight;
Each was clear to sight,
But they did not speak.

Then, a little sad,
Came my child in turn,
But the lamp he had,
Oh! it did not burn;
He, to clear my doubt,
Said, half turned about,
'Your tears put it out;
Mother, never mourn.'

For the Dorset original, see p. 226.

Melhill Feast

Aye up at the feast, by Melhill's brow,
So softly below the clouds in flight,
There swept on the wood, the shade and light,
Tree after tree, and bough by bough.

And there, as among the crowd, I took
My wandering way, both to and fro,
Full comely were shapes that day could show,
Face upon face, and look by look.

And there, among girls on left and right,
On one with a winsome smile, I set
My looks; and the more, the more we met
Glance upon glance, and sight by sight.

The road she had come by then was soon
The one of my paths that best I knew,
By glittering gossamer and dew,
Evening by evening, moon by moon.

First by the door of maidens fair,
As fair as the best till she is nigh,
Though now I can heedless pass them by,
One after one, or pair by pair.

Then by the orchards dim and cool,
And then along Woodcombe's timber'd side,
And then by the meads, where waters glide
Shallow by shallow, pool by pool.

And then to the house that stands alone
With roses around the porch and wall,
Where, up by the bridge, the waters fall
Rock under rock, and stone by stone.

Sweet were the hopes I found to cheer
My heart as I thought on time to come,
With one that would bless my happy home,
Moon upon moon, and year by year.

A Brisk Wind

The burdock leaves beside the ledge,
The leaves upon the poplar's height,
Were blown by windblasts up on edge,
And show'd their undersides of white;
And willow trees beside the rocks,
All bent grey leaves, and swung grey boughs,
As there, on wagging heads, dark locks
Bespread red cheeks, behung white brows.

Shellbrook

When out by Shellbrook, round by stile and tree,
With longer days and sunny hours come on,
With spring and all its sunny showers come on,
With May and all its shining flowers come on,
How merry, young with young would meet in glee.

And there, how we in merry talk went by
The foam below the river bay, all white,
And blossom on the green-leav'd may, all white,
And chalk beside the dusty way, all white,
Where glitt'ring water match'd with blue the sky.

Or else in winding paths and lanes, along
The timb'ry hillocks, sloping steep, we roam'd;
Or down the dells and dingles deep we roam'd;
Or by the bending brook's wide sweep we roam'd
On holidays, with merry laugh or song.

But now, the frozen churchyard wallings keep
The patch of tower-shaded ground, all white,
Where friends can find the frosted mound, all white
With turfy sides upswelling round, all white
With young offsunder'd from the young in sleep.

By the Mill in Spring

With wind to blow, and streams to flow,
To flow along the gravel stone,
The waves were bright, the cliffs were white,
Were white before the evening sun,
Where shaken sedge would softly sigh,
As we, with windblown locks, went by.

As lambs would swing their tails, and spring;
And spring about the ground chalk white;
The smoke was blue, above the yew;
The yew beside your house in sight;
And wind would sing with sullen sound,
Against the tree beside the mound;

Where down at mill, the wheel was still,
Was still, and dripp'd with glitt'ring tears,
With dusty poll, up lane would stroll,
The miller's man with mill-stunn'd ears;
While weakly-wailing wind would swim,
By ground with ivied elm-trees dim.

My work and way may fail or fay,
Or fay as days may freeze or glow,
I'll try to bear my toil or care,
Or care, with either friend or foe,
If, after all, the evening tide
May bring me peace, where I abide.

234

Sing again Together

Since now, once more beside this mound,
We friends are here below the limes,
Come, let us try if we can sound
A song we sang in early times.

When out among the hay in mead,
Or o'er the fields, or down the lane,
Our Jenny's voice would gaily lead
The others, chiming strain by strain.

When roses' buds are all outblown,
The lilies' cups will open white,
When lilies' cups, at last, are flown,
The later pinks unfold to sight.

We learnt good songs that came out new,
But now are old among the young,
And, after we are gone, but few
Will know the songs that we have sung.

So let us sing another rhyme
On this old mound in summer time.

Season Tokens

The shades may show the time of day,
And flowers, how summer wanes away.

Where thyme on turfy banks may grow,
Or mallows, by the laneside ledge,
About the blue-barr'd gate, may show
Their grey-blue heads, beside the hedge,

235

Or where the poppy's scarlet crown
May nod by clover, dusky red,
Or where the field is ruddy brown,
By brooks, with shallow-water'd bed.

The shades may show the time of day,
And flow'rs, how summer wanes away.
Or, where the light of dying day,
May softly shine against the wall,
Below the sloping thatch, brown-grey,
Or over pale-green grass, may fall,
Or where, in fields that heat burns dry,
May show the thistle's purple studs,
Or beds of dandelions ply
Their stems with yellow fringèd buds.

There shades may show the time of day,
And flowers, how summer wanes away.

By Neighbours' Doors

As up on trees' high limbs,
The western sunshine glowed,
And down by river brims
The wind-blown ripples flowed,
There we did seek the tun
Where evening smoke rose grey,
While dells begun to miss the light of day.

The mother-holden child,
Before the gate, would spring,
And crow, and struggle wild
At sight of birds on wing;
And home-bound men would shout
And make their game, before
The girls come out in clusters at the door.

Then we'd a door where all
Might gather to their rest,
When pale-beam'd stars might fall
Above the red-sky'd west,
But now, from that old door
We all have taken flight,
And some no more can tell the day from night.

Between Haymaking and Harvest

(JOHN AND HIS FRIEND)

J. The sunsped hours, with wheeling shades,
Have warm'd, for month on month, the glades,
    Till now the summer wanes;
Though shadows quiver down below
The boughs, that lofty elm-trees throw
        Across the dusty lanes;
F.   and docks,
    With ruddy stems, have risen tall
Beside the cow-forsaken stall,
        All free of hoofy hocks.

J. Along the swath with even side,
The meadow flow'rs have fall'n and died,
        And wither'd, rustling dry;
And in between the hay-wale's backs,
The waggon wheels have cut their tracks,
With loads of hay built high,
F.   and bound,
    And ev'ry rick with peakèd crown,
Is now down-toned to yellow brown,
        And sunburnt, two-thirds round.

J. The clouds now ride at upper height,
Above the barley yellow white;
        By lane and hedge; along

237

The fields of wheat, that ripen red,
And slowly reel, with giddy head,
   In wind that streams full strong,
F.   by copse,
And grass-field, where the cows lie down
Among the bent-grass, ruddy brown,
   And thistles' purple tops.

J. So come while sheep, now shorn, may run
Clean white, below the yellow sun,
   In daisy beds; before
The swinging hook may come to shear
The yellow wheat with nodding ear,
   Come, welcome, to my door.
F.   I'll rest
Beside the clover-whiten'd knap,
With weary hand upon my lap,
   One day your happy guest.

On the Road

Still green on the limbs of the oak were the leaves,
Where the sloe daily grew, with its skin-bloom of grey,
Though in fields, summer-burnt, stood the bent-grass,
    well brown'd,
And the stubble of wheatfields was withering white,
While sooner the sunlight now sank from the sight,
And longer now linger'd the dim-roaded night.

But bright was the daylight that dried up the dew,
As the foam-water fill'd the wide pool in its fall,
And as I came to climb, by the chalk of the cliff,
The white road full steep to the wayfaring step,
Where along by the hill, with a high-beating breast,
Went the girl or the man to the feast in their best.

There the horse would prance by, with his neck a high
    bow,
And would toss up his nose over outspringing knees;
And the ox, with sleek hide, and with low-swimming
    head;
And the sheep, little kneed, with a quickdipping nod;
And a girl, with her head carried on in a proud
Gait of walking, as smooth as an air-swimming cloud.

The Knoll

(The speaker, who lives by the knoll, talks to an old friend

O home, people tell us, is home
        be it never so homely,
And Meldon 's the home where my fathers
        all sleep by the knoll.

And there they have left me a living,
        in land, where, in summer,
My hay, wither'd grey, awaits hauling
        in heap, by the knoll.

And there, among bright-shining grass-blades,
        and bent-grass, in autumn,
My cows may all lie near the waters
        that creep by the knoll,

And up on the slope of the hillocks,
        by white-rinded ash-trees,
Are ledges of grass and of thyme-beds,
        with sheep, by the knoll.

And down on the west of my house
        is a rookery, rocking
In trees that will ward off the winds
        that may sweep by the knoll.

And there I have windows outlooking
      to blushing-skied sunset,
And others that face the fresh morning's
      first peep, by the knoll.

And though there is no place but heaven
      without any sorrow,
And I, like my fellows in trial,
      may weep by the knoll,

Still, while I fulfil, like a hireling,
      the day of my labour,
I wish, if my wish is not sinful,
      to keep by the knoll.

So, if you can find a day empty
      of work, with fine weather,
And feel yourself willing to climb
      up the steep by the knoll,

Come up, and we'll make ourselves merry
      once more, all together;
You'll find that your bed and your board
      shall be cheap by the knoll.

Hill and Dell[1]

At John's, up on Sandhills, 'tis healthy and dry,
Though I may not like it, it may be—not I.
Where fir-trees are spindling, with tapering tops,
From leafy-leav'd fern in the cold stunted copse,
And under keen gorsebrakes, all yellow in bloom,
The skylark's brown nest is deep-hidden in gloom;

---

[1] For the Dorset original, see p. 263.

240

And high on the cliff, where no foot ever wore
A path to the threshold, 's the sandmartin's door,
On waterless heights, while the winds lowly sigh,
On tree-climbing ivy, before the blue sky.

I think I could hardly like his place as well
As my own shelter'd home in the timbery dell,
Where rooks come to build in the high-swaying
    boughs,
And broadheaded oaks yield a shade for the cows;
Where grey-headed withy-trees lean o'er the brook
Of grey-lighted waters that whirl by the nook,
And only the girls and the swans are in white,
Like snow on grey moss in the midwinter's light,
And wind softly drives, with a low rustling sound,
By waves on the water and grass on the ground.

The Shop of Meat-ware, or Wares to Eat

(The complaint of a housemother who keeps a huxter's shop)

By selling meat-ware I shall get no meat;
I must not keep a shop of wares to eat.
I have some goods, but I can hardly think
That they are sold as quickly as they shrink;
I have some goods, but yet my little stocks
Will waste away, like camphor in a box.
Some hand, at whiles, steals in, and slily slips
Some little thing away for some two lips.
You people here don't wait for gain of trade,
But take the store before the gain is made.
I had some eggs, and I can miss some eggs,
And I don't think they went without some legs.
I had some eggs, and some have left my store,
And I don't think they travell'd out of door;
I had some eggs, and eggs have gone from hence,

241

And I don't think they brought me any pence;
I had some eggs, as yet I know full well;
I bought some eggs, but now have none to sell.

Air and Light

Ah! look and see how widely free
    O'er all the land the wind will spread;
If here a tree-top sways, a tree
    On yonder hillock waves its head.
How wide the light outshows to sight
The place and living face of man?
How far the river runs for lip
To drink, or hand to sink and dip.

But one may sink with sudden woe
    That may not pass, in wider flight,
To other souls, declining slow,
    And hush'd, like birds at fall of night.
And some are sad, while some are glad;
In turn we all may mourn our lot:
And days that come in joy may go
In evenings sad with heavy woe.

The morning sun may cast abroad
    His light on dew about our feet,
And down below his noontide road
    The streams may glare below his heat;
The evening light may sparkle bright
Across the quiv'ring gossamer;
But I, though fair he still may glow,
Must miss a face he cannot show.

Written 15th April 1864

The Fireside Chairs

HUSBAND TO WIFE

The daylight gains upon the night,
And birds are out in later flight;
'Tis cold enough to spread our hands,
Once now and then, to glowing brands.
So now we two are here alone
To make a quiet hour our own,
We'll take, with face to face, once more
Our places on the warm hearth floor,
Where you shall have the window view
Outside, and I can look on you.

When first I brought you home, my bride,
In yellow glow of summer tide,
I wanted you to take a chair
On that side of the fire—out there—
And have the ground and sky in sight,
With face against the window light;
While I, back here, should have my brow
In shade, and sit where I am now;
That you might see the land outside,
And I might look on you, my bride.

And there the gliding waters spread,
By waving elm-trees over head,
Below the hill that slopes above
The path, along the high-treed grove,
Where sighing winds once whisper'd down
Our whisper'd words; and there's the crown
Of *Duncliffe* hill, where widening shades
Of timber fall on sloping glades:
So you enjoy the green and blue
Without, and I will look on you.

And there we pull'd, within the copse,
With nutting-crooks the hazel tops,
That now arise, unleaved and black,
Too thin to keep the wind-blast back;
And there's the church, and spreading lime,
Where we did meet at evening time,
In clusters, on the beaten green,
In glee, to see and to be seen;
All old sights, welcomer than new,
And look'd on, as I look'd on you.

Black and White

By the wall of the garden that glimmer'd, chalk white,
In the light of the moon, back in May,
There were you all in black, at my side, coming round
On the ground where the cypress did sway:
Oh! the white and the black. Which was fairest to view?
Why the black, become fairest on you.

By the water downfalling in many a bow,
White as snow, on the rock's peaky steep;
There your own petted cow show'd the ridge of her
    back,
Of deep black, as she lay for her sleep:
Oh! the white and the black. Which was fairest to view?
Why the black, become fairest on you.

When you stroll'd down the village at evening, bedight
All in white, in the warm summer-tide,
The while *Towsy*, your loving old dog, with his back
Sleeky black, trotted on at your side:
Ah! the black and the white. Which was fairest to view?
Why the white, become fairest on you.

At the end of the barton the granary stood,
Of black wood, with white geese at its side;
And the white-wingèd swans, on the quick-running
    wave,
By the cave of black darkness did glide:
Oh! the black and the white. Which was fairest to view?
Why the white, become fairest on you.

Bed-ridden

The sun may in glory go by,
   Though by cloudiness hidden from sight;
And the moon may be bright in the sky,
   Though an air-mist may smother its light.
There is joy in the world among some,
   And among them may joy ever be;
And oh! is there health-joy to come,
   Come any more unto me?

The stream may be running its way,
   Under ice that lies dead as the stone,
And below the dark water may play
   The quick fishes in swimmings unshown,
There is sprightliness shown among some,
   Aye, and sprightly may they ever be,
And oh! is there limb-strength to come,
   Come any more unto me?

Plorata Veris Lacrimis

O now, my true and dearest bride,
Since thou hast left my lonely side,
My life has lost its hope and zest.
The sun rolls on from east to west,

But brings no more that evening rest,
Thy loving-kindness made so sweet,
And time is slow that once was fleet,
    As day by day was waning.

The last sad day that show'd thee lain
Before me, smiling in thy pain,
The sun soar'd high along his way
To mark the longest summer day,
And show to me the latest play
Of thy sweet smile, and thence, as all
The days' lengths shrunk from small to small,
    My joy began its waning.

And now 'tis keenest pain to see
Whate'er I saw in bliss with thee.
The softest airs that ever blow,
The fairest days that ever glow,
Unfelt by thee, but bring me woe.
And sorrowful I kneel in pray'r,
Which thou no longer, now, canst share,
    As day by day is waning.

How can I live my lonesome days?
How can I tread my lonesome ways?
How can I take my lonesome meal?
Or how outlive the grief I feel?
Or how again look on to weal?
Or sit, at rest, before the heat
Of winter fires, to miss thy feet,
    When evening light is waning.

Thy voice is still I lov'd to hear,
Thy voice is lost I held so dear.
Since death unlocks thy hand from mine,
No love awaits me such as thine;
Oh! boon the hardest to resign!

But if we meet again at last
In heav'n, I little care how fast
          My life may now be waning.

1852

Do Good

Ah! child! the stream that brings
  To thirsty lips their drink,
Is seldom drain'd; for springs
  Pour water to its brink.

The wellsprings that supply
  The streams, are seldom spent,
For clouds of rain come by
  To pay them what they lent.

The clouds that cast their rain
  On lands that yield our food,
Have water from the main,
  To make their losses good.

The sea is paid by lands,
  With streams from ev'ry shore;
So give with kindly hands,
  For God can give you more.

He would that in a ring
  His blessings should be sent,
From living thing to thing,
  But nowhere staid or spent.

And ev'ry soul that takes,
  But yields not on again,
Is so a link that breaks
  In Heaven's love-made chain.

FROM

A SELECTION

FROM UNPUBLISHED POEMS

BY THE REV. WILLIAM BARNES

1870

Musings

Before the falling summer sun
   The boughs are shining all as gold,
And down below them waters run,
   As there in former years they roll'd;
The poolside wall is glowing hot,
   The pool is in a dazzling glare,
And makes it seem as, ah! 'tis not,
   A summer when my life was fair,

The evening, gliding slowly by,
   Seems one of those that long have fled;
The night comes on to star the sky
   As then it darken'd round my head.
A girl is standing by yon door,
   As one in happy times was there,
And this day seems, but is no more,
   A day when all my life was fair.

We hear from yonder feast the hum
   Of voices, as in summers past;
And hear the beatings of the drum
   Again come throbbing on the blast.
There neighs a horse in yonder plot,
   As once there neigh'd our petted mare,
And summer seems, but ah! is not
   The summer when our life was fair.

Flowers a-Field

In hay-fields where the hedge-boughs cope
The sunny hedge-bank's flow'ry slope,
Out where the prickly wildrose blows,
Above the bloomy bramble-bows,

Some maiden cries 'The briars prick
My fingers to the very quick;
Come pull me down a wild rose, do,
For I can't cope with it like you!'

And out in meadows, where the hay,
Now nearly dry, is rustling gray,
Before the touch of rake or prongs,
And under women's merry songs;
Then there, as I by chance come by
The laughing girls, I hear them cry,
'Come pull me down a woodbine, do,
For I can't reach it there. Can you?'

And down beside the river's brim,
Where swirling waters softly swim—
Where we can see the bulrush nod
Its club upon its slender rod;
Then there, as merry girls behold
The water-lily's flow'r of gold,
They cry, 'Oh! rake me out one, do,
For I can't reach it in. Can you?'

Cliffwood

By Cliffwood rocks I took my way
 With sorrow-sunken mind,
As slowly waned the ling'ring day
 To labour-worn mankind.
No shadow fell on slope or dell,
 'Twas sunless, though not wet;
The sun was clouded off to me,
 I saw not where it set.

I pass'd the lawn where once I sought
  My joy at Mary's door,
And where I linger'd still in thought,
  When I was there no more.
For while all gay in merry play,
  We there at evening met,
Unheeded sank the hornèd moon,
  I saw not where it set.

I came from foreign lands, once more
  By that dear way to roam;
But she's no longer at her door,
  She's at a better home.
That she had lain one day in pain
  No tidings did I get;
My sun went down unknown to me,
  I knew not when it set.

Arise, O Winds!

Arise, O winds, and drive away
  The curling fog by mound or nook,
For we to-day would see you play
  Along the lightly-sparkling brook.
    By brook and brake,
    O winds, awake.

Arise! but do not mar our way
  With clouds of dust to blind our eyes,
For we would look this holiday
  On all the charms of land and skies.
    By hill and lake,
    O winds, awake.

O winds, blow on! but do not fly
   With dark'ning clouds of sudden show'rs,
For we would pass the fields all dry
   Among the heads of summer flow'rs.
      Sweep hill and plain,
      But not with rain.

And come to-night to clear away
   The clouds that o'er the moon may pass,
For we may wish to see you play
   By moonshades on the beech-side grass.
      So make, we pray,
      A happy day.

Time Steals Away

Ay! if you mark the sunny ground,
   Where now the maypole shade may fall,
It soon will wheel a span around,
   While seeming not to go at all.
I know not how the time is flown
   Since you and I met here one May;
A day of rest, a season blest,
   For oh! how time will steal away.

While once our evening mirth began,
   The candle's glossy stem was tall,
But soon burnt down, a long half-span,
   Though seeming not to sink at all.
The time is gone, I know not how,
   Since there we gather'd, young and gay,
In nights of joys, with merry noise,
   For oh! how lifetime steals away.

The winterbourne, when o'er the dell
   The spring was green, was flowing fast,
And then fell dry, but who can tell
   What day and hour it ran its last.
I know not how the time has fled
   Since there, with you, I flung the hay,
In youth's gay pride, in hope's fair tide,
   For oh! how lifetime steals away.

As when the ship goes under sail
   Far out before the sounding beach,
And, while we hear some friend's new tale,
   She sinks beyond our eyesight's reach.
So time has gone, I know not how,
   Since we had picnics on the bay,
The happy year, the summer dear,
   Of time that softly steals away.

Proud of his Home

Up under the wood, where treetips sway
All green, though by skyshine tinted gray;
Above the soft mead, where waters glide,
Here narrow and swift, there slow and wide,
Up there is my house, with rose-trimm'd walls,
By land that up-slopes, and land that falls—
On over the mill, and up on the ridge,
Up on the ledge above the bridge.

The wind, as it comes along the copse,
Is loud with the rustling trees' high tops;
The wind from beyond the brook is cool,
And sounds of the ever-whirling pool:
Up there at my house, with well-trimmed thatch,
And lowly-wall'd lawn, and archèd hatch,

Beside the tall trees where blackbirds sing—
Over the rock, and water spring.

And when from the north the wind blows cold,
The trees are my screen, a hundred fold;
And wind that may blow from southern skies,
Through quivering limetrees softly sighs,
And out in the west a tow'r stands gray,
And hills on the eastward fade away—
From under the wood, above the mill,
Over the stream, below the hill.

As people along the road go by,
They suddenly turn their heads awry,
They slacken their canter to a trot,
With 'Oh! what a pretty little spot!'
They take for their trot a walking pace,
With 'Heigh! what a charming little place!'
They lift up their hands with wond'ring look,
With 'Lo! what a lovely little nook!'

They see my laburnums' chains of gold,
And pallid blue lilac flow'rs unfold;
They look at my fuchsias' hanging bells,
And calceolarias' yellow shells,
And cups of my lilies, white as snow,
And pinks as they hang their blossoms low;
And then at my roses, fine and fair
As ever have sweeten'd summer air.

They look at my rose with open eyes,
With 'Oh! what a handsome shape and size;'
They put up their hand to breast or hair,
To fancy they put my rose up there;
They put up a leaf below the nose,
To fancy they smell my fine moss-rose;
With back-looking face they go their ways,
With 'Oh! that's the place that people praise'.

The foot-weary man that there may tread
The road, with no place to lay his head,
Will say, as he heaves his sighing breast,
'How blest is the man with that sweet nest!'
And bachelors fain would own the care
Of sweet little children playing there—
Up under the wood, on Meldon ridge,
Up the road, from Meldon bridge.

How Great Become

How great do I become! How great!
   With all my children now full grown,
And settled, each a wedded mate,
   And all with children of their own.
I first was one, and then one more
   Well-wived; and children made me ten;
   And they with all their wives or men,
And children, now make me two score,
   With children's children, far or nigh,
   How great I am become! Am I?

I own a share of Weston folk,
   On Norton work I have some hands,
At Beechley I send up a smoke,
   My surname sounds on Ashridge lands.
In Meldon church my voices sing,
   Yes, there I have young tongues to pray,
   And I have boys and girls at play
Below the rocks, at Clevewell spring.
   With all the souls that I may claim
   How great I am! How great my name!

But oh! how little can I track
   The longsome team of father men,

That runs, from me to elders, back
　　A chain of links beyond my ken.
O'er what dear heads, by one and one,
　　My name at length came down on me
　　I know not now, nor may I see
Below me one child's child's sweet son.
　　No. I am only one of all
　　Those links of life. But one. How small!

The Rooks

Ay! when the sun is near the ground,
　　At evening, in the western sky,
From west to eastward, all around,
　　The gathered rooks begin to fly.

In wedgelike flock, with one ahead,
　　They flap their glitt'ring wings in flight;
But did you ever hear it said
　　Whereto they take their way at night!

At Akdean wood, folk say they meet,
　　To fold at night their weary wings,
And roost, with little clenching feet,
　　On boughs that nightwind softly swings.

O yes, at Akdean's shadowy ground
　　Are broad limb'd oaks, and ashes tall;
Black pines, and aspen trees that sound
　　As soft as water at a fall.

There I have spent some happy hours,
　　Where yellow sunshine broke through shades
On blue-bell beds and cowslip flow'rs,
　　And us among them, in the glades.

A Night Song, No. 1

Oh! do you wake, or do you sleep
   With window to the full-moon'd sky?
Oh! have you lost, or do you keep
   A thought of all the day gone by?
Or are you dead to all you knew
Of life, the while I live to you?

May air, o'er wallside roses brought,
   Of charming gardens give you dreams;
May rustling leaves beguile your thought
   With dreams of walks by falling streams.
And on your lids be light that yields
Bright dream-clouds over daisied fields.

Our meeting hour of yesterday
   To me, now deep in waning night,
Seems all a glory pass'd away
   Beyond a year-time's longsome flight.
Though night seems far too short to weigh
Your words and deeds of yesterday.

While rise or sink the glittering stars
   Above dim woods, or hillock brows,
There, out within the moonpaled bars,
   In darksome bunches sleep your cows.
So sweetly sleep, asleep be they
Until you meet the opening day.

A Night Song, No. 2

Be it midnight, be it dawning,
   Do the clouds hold up, or weep;
Be it moonlight, be it sunshine,
   Is no care to folk asleep.

259

So I linger not to tell you
　　How the midnight moon may soar;
But if one thing be your business,
　　'Tis that love is at the door.

Whether leafy is the chestnut,
　　Or its chilly twigs be bare;
Whether dewy, whether frosty
　　Be the grass, is not your care.
So forget until the morning,
　　Land below, and sky above;
But it should be worth your knowing,
　　That before your gate is love.

Oh! how softly in our slumbers
　　Do we oft, unwitting, glide
From the day's end to the morrow,
　　Over midnight's gloomy tide.
So may every day that opens,
　　Bring to you its one joy more,
Till you live in peace and honour,
　　Blest with love within my door.

Like a birdling, say the people,
　　Is young Love, that fain would roam,
Ever lively in his freedom,
　　But will die confined at home.
No. I feel that you will never
　　Find the love at my heart's core,
Flying, faithless, out of window
　　Though stern want should come to door.

FROM

POEMS AND FRAGMENTS
HITHERTO UNCOLLECTED

(The dates are of publication in the *Dorset
County Chronicle*)

Hill or Dell[1]

At John's, up on zand-hill, 'tis heathy an' dry
Though I midden like it i' may be, not I.
Where vir-trees do spindle, wi' teäperèn tops,
Vrom leafy-leav'd vern, in the cwold-stunted copse,
An' under sharp vuzzen, all yollow in blooth,
The sky-lark's brown nest is a-hid in the lewth,
An' high on the cliff, where noo voot ever wore
A path to the drashold, 's the zandmartin's door,
On waterless heights, where the wind do stream by
A-sighèn by ivy, avore the blue sky.
I do think I could teäke vor the best o' the two
My timber-screen'd hwome, here below in the lew;
Where rooks be a-buildèn in high elem boughs,
An' broadheaded woaks be a-sheäde vor the cows,
Where greyheaded withies do leän by the feäce
O' greylighted waters, a-slacknèn their peäce,
An' only the maïdens an' swans be in white,
Like snow on grey moss in the mid-winter's light,
An' wind do dreve on, wi' a low-ruslen sound
By weäves on the water, an grass on the ground.

My Love a-Growen

(From a Tuscan folk-poem)

As vrom the pond's lew zide the weäves do zwim
Vrom small to bigger, to the windy brim,
As winds in yonder woods do murmur low,
And higher sound, the nearer they do blow,
As day a-breakèn to the mornèn moon
Do grow in brightness to the burnèn noon,

[1] The English version is printed on p. 240.

Zoo grew my love, vrom small to woman high,
Vrom feäir to feäirer, as the years went by,
Zoo did my love to woman's height vrom small
Grow feäirer, year by year, a-growèn tall.
Vrom small to women-high, my love did show
Mwore comely, and my love wi' her did grow.

The Hearth of Urien

(From the Elegy on Urien attributed to the bard
Llywarch the Aged)

Is not this hearth, where goats now feed?
Here chatt'ring tongues, with noisy speed,
Once talk'd around the yellow mead.

Is not this hearth this day among
Tall nettles? Once here stood a throng
Of Owen's suitors all day long.

Is not this hearth with grass o'erspread?
Ere noble Owen yet was dead,
The cauldron-heating flames were red.

Is not this hearth where toad-stools grow?
There Owen's warriors once did show
The swordblade dreaded by the foe.

Is not this hearth within a band
Of rushes? Once here blazed the brand,
And food was dealt with lib'ral hand.

Is not this hearth below the thorn?
Here, ere it thus was left forlorn,
Did once pass round the mead's deep horn.

Is not this hearth where emmets crawl?
Here blazed the torch upon the wall,
Around the crowded banquet hall.

264

Is not this hearth now cold among
Red sorrel-stems? Here once a throng
Of warriors drank with laugh and song.

Is not this hearth, where swine have plough'd?
Here once bold warriors' tongues were loud,
As mead-cups pass'd among the crowd.

Is not this hearth, where scrapes the hen?
No want was here among the men
Of brave Owen and Urien.

1863

Cynddylan's Hall

(From the Elegy on Cynddylan attributed to the bard
Llywarch the Aged)

Cynddylan's hall is all in gloom—to-night;
No fire, no lighted room:
Amid the stillness of a tomb.

Cynddylan's hall is left alone—to-night:
A hall with none to own.
O Death, take me where he is flown.

Cynddylan's hall is now unblest—to-night;
On Hydwyrth's rocky crest
No lord is there, no meal, no guest.

Cynddylan's hall! It makes me wan
To see cold hearths and roofing gone.
My lord is dead, and I live on!

Cynddylan's hall is sad within—to-night;
For sons of Cyndrwyn,
Cynon, Gwion, and Gwyn.

1867

An Englyn on a Yellow Greyhound

(From the *Englyn i Vilgi Melyn*, in Edward Jones's 'Musical
and Poetical Relicks of the Welsh Bards' 1794)

Hound yellow, light of tread—the cunning foe
Of deer bedappled red;
He of the wind gets not ahead,
Nor yet is by the wind outsped.

1867

The Dove

(From *Bugeilgerrd*—'Pastoral Poem'—by Edward Richard
1714–1777)

I once in happy times
Within my leafy grove,
With joyful voice did rove
And with the cuckoo sing
And now am like a dove
That in his grief alone
Upon some beam may moan
The losing of a wing.

The Storm-Wind

When the swift-rolling brook, swollen deep,
Rushes on by the alders, full speed,
And the wild-blowing winds lowly sweep
O'er the quivering leaf and the weed,
And the willow tree writhes in each limb,
Over sedge-beds that reel by the brim—

The man that is staggering by
Holds his hat to his head by the brim;

266

And the girl as her hair-locks outfly,
   Puts a foot out, to keep herself trim,
And the quivering wavelings o'erspread
The small pool where the bird dips his head.

But out at my house, in the lee
   Of the nook, where the winds die away,
The light swimming airs, round the tree
   And the low-swinging ivy stem, play
So soft that a mother that's nigh
Her still cradle, may hear her babe sigh.

1868

Troubles of the Day

As there, along the elmy hedge, I go
   By banksides white with parsley—parsley-bloom—
Where smell of new-mown hay comes wafted by
   On wind of dewy evening, evening gloom,
And homeward take my shaded way between
The hedge's high-tipp'd wood, and barley green,
      I sing, or mean
'O troubles of the day, flee to the west,
Come not my homeward way. I seek my rest.'

The dairy cows, by meadow trees, lie free,
   Of calls to milkers' pails—the milkmaids' calls;
The horses now have left their rolling wheels
   And reel'd in home to stable, to their stalls,
And down the grey-pool'd stream the fish awhile
Are free from all the prowling angler's guile,
      And o'er the stile
I sink, and sing or say, 'Flee to the west,
O troubles of the day. I seek my rest.'

My boy—whose little high-rigged boat, athwart
  The windy pool, by day, at afternoon,
Has fluttered, tippling like a bird
  That tries to fly unfledged, to fly too soon—
Now sleeps forgetful of the boat, and fond
Old dog that he has taught to swim the pond.
     So flee beyond
The edge of sinking day, towards the west,
Ye troubles, flee away. I seek my rest.

A star is o'er the tower on the hill
  Whence rings no clanging knell, no evening peal;
The mill stands dark beside the flouncing foam,
  But still is all its gear, its mossy wheel.
No rooks now sweep along the darkened sky,
And o'er the road few feet or wheels go by.
     So fly, O fly
Ye troubles, with the day, adown the west,
Come not along my way. I seek my rest.

1869

The Moor

Where yonder leaning hill-side roves
  With woody dippings, far around
And many jutting brows, and coves,
  Of rugged cliffs, and slopy ground,
Beside the stream that slowly sinks
    With reaches tinted from the skies,
    And stream-side meadows, lowly lies
The moor, with dikes and sedgy brinks.

About us there the willow shade
  Oft play'd beside the water's edge,
And there the rodded bulrush sway'd
  Its soft brown club, above the sedge.

268

And by the aspen or the bridge,
    The angler sat, and lightly whipp'd
    His little float, that, dancing, dipp'd
From o'er the waveling's little ridge.

There cows, in clusters, rambled wide,
  Some hanging low their heads to eat,
Some lying on their heavy side,
  Some standing on their two-peaked feet,
Some sheeted white, some dun or black,
    Some red, and others brindled dark,
    Some marked with milk-white star, or spark,
And ours all white along the back.

There cows, to others, low'd; now here
Now there, from open heat to shade;
And out among them, far or near,
  With quiv'ring scream, the horses neigh'd
The while some boy, within the mead,
    On some high mare might come astride;
    And sliding down her bulging side,
Might set her, snorting, free to feed.

And there we saw the busy crow
  For mussels down the river play,
And rooks sweep on where men below
  Went, water-hemm'd, their crooked way,
And gamb'ling boys, in merry train,
    On holidays came rambling by
    With often-grounded poles, to fly
In high-bow'd flight, o'er dike and drain.

There men at work on pathless grass,
  Are seen, though out of hearing wide,
By neighbour-meeting folk, that pass
  The many-roaded upland side.

So some may like the trampled road,
   O'er well-rubbed stile-bars, with a gloss,
   And some the moor, that some may cross
But pass no door of man's abode.

1869

Leaf Hues

Where green is all the common hue
   Of leaves, there seldom comes to light
A greenness for the blossoms too;
   But they are blue, or red, or white.

With my dear child's last dress of green
   Her face of blushing white was seen;
The while her hair hung freely down
   In waving locks of golden brown.

The chestnut leaves die off to red,
   And maple leaves in yellow die;
The holly leaves in brown lie dead,
   And bramble brown and gray will die.

But she lay dead as white's a sheet;
   She lay as white as flour of wheat;
And she was folded all in white,
   To rise an angel ever bright.

1869

Sister Gone

When Mary on her wedding day,
At last a bride, had gone away
From all her friends that there had spent
The happy day in merriment,

270

And ringers rang, at evenfall,
Their peals of bells, from great to small,
Within the tower's mossy wall
So high against the evening sky.

Then Jane, that there throughout the day
Had been the gayest of the gay,
At last began to hang her head
And ponder on her sister fled,
And days that seem'd too quickly flown,
To leave her now at home alone,
With no one's life to match her own,
So sad, though hitherto so glad.

It saddened me that moonpaled night
To see her by the wall, in white,
While friends departed mate with mate
Beyond the often-swinging gate,
As there beside the lilac shade,
Where golden-chained laburnum sway'd,
Around her face her hairlocks play'd,
All black with light behind her back.

1869.

First Shown

With you first shown to me,
With you first known to me,
My life-time loom'd, in hope, a length of joy:
Your voice so sweetly spoke,
Your mind so meetly spoke,
My hopes were all of bliss without alloy,
As I, for your abode, sought out, with pride,
This house with vines o'er-rangling all its side.

I thought of years to come,
All free of tears to come,
When I might call you mine, and mine alone,
With steps to fall for me,
And daycares all for me,
And hands for ever nigh to help my own;
And then thank'd Him who had not cast my time
Too early or too late for your sweet prime.

Then bright was dawn, o'er dew,
And day withdrawn, o'er dew,
And mid-day glow'd on flow'rs along the ledge,
And walls in sight, afar,
Were shining white, afar,
And brightly shone the stream beside the sedge.
But still, the fairest light of those clear days
Seem'd that which fell along your flow'ry ways.

1869

Older

(Husband and Wife)

H. As golden chains behung their tree
And swung, in breezes, to and fro,
There you, below the humming bee,
Were sitting in the shade to sew.

W. Ah! sew in white, with no black dyes
Of mourning, under weeping eyes.

H. With eyes that show'd a glist'ning blue
As clear as succory blossoms bear,
Or as your girdle, shining new,
Or knot new-made for breast or hair.

272

W. Aye, hair, all glossy black, that all
　　Now withers grey in life's late fall.

H. Yet fall, with charms we all can feel,
　　　Awaits the ripening time and sun,
　　For gifts, enhancing all our weal,
　　　In growth of fruits by spring begun.

W. Begun, as once with us begun
　　Our life that now is far outrun.

H. Outrun to reach a happy stage
　　　To which our riper mind has brought
　　A treasure for our wiser age,
　　　The wisdom cull'd from time by thought.

1869

A Bride Song

　　The bride forsakes her maiden room,
　　　And window up below the eaves,
　　And now, O merry birds, to whom
　　　Will ye all sing among the leaves?
　　Go call the dove from woods aloof
　　To moan in trees above her roof.

　　The bride has left her mother's door
　　　Nor soon again shall there be shown;
　　Oh! sweep ye not the hallowed floor,
　　　Oh! sweep ye not the threshold stone,
　　For fear ye heedlessly offsweep
　　Her tracks that all the ground should keep.

　　The bride has left the garden hatch,
　　　To let her through it swung about;
　　Turn not to-night its key or latch,

273

As if you meant to shut her out,
Nor while the wicket keepeth good
Give to the fire its hallow'd wood.

The bride is gone along the road,
    And with her joy is gone away;
Oh! bless her to her new abode,
    Though dull be left your lonesome day.
Her road was to the western sky,
Where now your thoughts will daily fly.

1871

Not to be Forgotten

Oh! that days should follow on
    Until at last, to all mankind,
Your shape and name should all be gone
    Both out of sight and out of mind,
That every thought of you should die,
    And be forgotten ev'rywhere,
As that of bloom or butterfly
    That shines a little while so fair.
        Oh! that I could somehow set you
        So that man should not forget you.

Aye, could I for ever leave
    Your name on yonder spring or rill,
Or give it evermore to cleave
    To yonder everlasting hill;
Or make the hollow rocks a tongue
    To sound it with the wind in flight,
Or find some fairy, ever young,
    To give it on in dreams of night.
        Oh! that I could somehow set it
        Where the world should not forget it.

274

Somehow set your shape and hue
  On time-proof stone that nought could mar,
To last as if for ever new,
  As in the sky abides the star;
Or could but find in my sweet thought
  Of you, sweet wording for the tongue
Of song, that ever should be caught
  From all the old, by all the young—
     Song that should for ever set you
     Where the world should not forget you.

1872

Not Sing at Night

While sang the lark above the lea,
Or thrush by neshleav'd bush or tree,
In early day, or afternoon,
We often heard the merry tune
Of your gay song from orchard shades
Or bough-hemm'd lanes, or grassy glades,
But hardly ever found you trill
A song at night, when birds were still.

The way the merry sound came by
Betoken'd, what I fain would spy,
Your steps behind some half-brown'd rick,
Or flow'ry hedge, too high and thick,
Or where below the clear blue sky
The snow-white linen hung to dry,
But where you would not go to fill
The shade with sound when birds were still.

When darkness dimm'd the hues of day,
And we went lonely on the way
Without the day's high noises near,
We there, upon the road, could hear

275

Beside the grey old bars the sound
Of barley rustling o'er the ground,
But never found your warbling come
Upon the wind, when birds were dumb.

When clouds bedimm'd the welkin's blue,
And night came on without its dew,
And winter wind had stripp'd the trees,
And crackling roads began to freeze,
And ground erst warm with summer heat
Was whiten'd o'er with happ'ring sleet,
You sang where I would fain have heard
You, still at home, while sang no bird.

1872

Rooks and Swallows

I sat me where an ash tree's head
  From o'er a bankside reach'd around,
With outcast shade that overspread
  Some grass, and eke some stubbled ground,
While hedges up the hillock's brows
Held out their now befruited boughs.

The children and the birds well knew
  Where hung the berried bramble bows,
Or where were sloes of mealy blue,
  Or heps, the children of the rose,
Or elderberries over head
Were black, or boughs of haws were red.

There near the wheatrick's yellow back,
  That shone like gold before the sky,
Some rooks with wings of glossy black
  Came on down wheeling from on high,
And lightly pitched upon their feet
Among the stubble of the wheat.

And then some swallows floated by,
   All sweeping out their airy bow,
And rising up from low to high,
   Or sweeping down from high to low,
Now soon to strike their longer flight,
Away from our land's chilly light.

'The rooks,' I thought, 'will still behold,
   These trees, leafbare, in driven sleet,
The swallows shun our winter cold
   For clearer skies and glowing heat.
And which is best? To have no year
Of home, or lifelong dwelling here?'

On sunny days we often yearn
   To speed us to some other land,
And men of other tongues, and learn
   Their ways of life, and works of hand;
Aye, how the world of lands is fill'd
With many menkinds many-skilled.

But since we lack the wings of gold
   That waft men over all the earth,
And find our livelihood withhold
   Our life to this our land of birth;
So let it be, since like a dove
We find us here enough to love.

1872

The Old Farmhouse

That many-tunn'd farmhouse that stands
   A little off the old high road,
When landlords lived upon their lands,
   Was long its landlord's dear abode;

277

And often thence, with horn-call'd hounds
 High-steeded through the gate he sped,
The while the whirring grey-wing'd doves
 Flew out of dovecoats overhead.

And after that, below the tun,
 There burnt for happy souls the fire
Of one whose name has blest his son,
 A farmer fit to be a squire.
And while his barley-sowing sped,
 On dusty mould, in springtide light,
From those old dovecotes' many doors
 The grey-wing'd doves arose in flight.

And while through days of longsome span
 His corn was sunn'd from green to red,
His son grew up from boy to man,
 And now is master in his stead;
For him the loaded waggons roll
 To staddled ricks that rustle dry,
And there for him the grey-wing'd doves
 Around the mossy dovecots fly.

There oft his sister, then a child—
 That's now a mother, fair, though staid—
His merry playmate flitted wild
 And tittering, through light and shade
On tiptoe, fanning in her speed
 The gold-like straws beside her shoe;
While to the dovecotes, nigh at hand,
 The grey-wing'd doves in haste upflew.

And still with fondness, and with praise
 The brother's and the sister's mind
Behold their home-spent childhood's days
 So fair, and left so far behind—

As I behold, in thought, the time
    When first the lord of wall and sward
There dwelt, and first the grey-wing'd doves
    Flew out from dovecotes in the yard.

1873

Return

If a leaf swim away on the stream,
    Who can tell where 'twill rest at the last?
Or if thistledown fly on the wind
    Will it come by a back-flowing blast?
If my love o'er the ocean shall roam
Will he come again home,
                Aye, home?

Shall the fleet-rushing swallow that speeds
    In the fall o'er the broad-reaching sea,
Come again in the following spring,
    Here to wheel round the old parrock tree?
If my love sail afar from the land
Will he yet shake our hand,
                Aye, hand?

Oh! the cherry-tree blossom'd all white,
    And again with its cherries was red;
But it now has been chill'd by the frost,
    And it seems to be withering dead.
I had joy under last summer's sky,
And to-year must it die,
                Aye, die?

No. My love's not a leaf on the stream,
    Nor the down of the thistle's brown seeds,
Nor a swallow that never may find
    Its old haunts in our green summer meads.

And although for a while he may roam,
He will find his way home,
                        Aye, home.

1875

Hiding my Love

(From a Tuscan folk-poem)

I wish that all the crooked streets were gone,
And ev'ry house had fasten'd up its door;
And all the hills were levell'd as a floor,
That hide a shape so fair to look upon.
I wish that ev'ry oak would die and fall,
That bears a hanging leaf, however small,
That bears a single leaf, which, hanging low,
May hide my love, on walking to and fro.

1875

A Rejection

(From a Tuscan folk-poem)

Bloom of the cypress tree.
    I write with one hand, and with one erase,
I must confess I do not care for thee.

Violets quickly fade.
    Full oft to me my mother dear has said
Men seek the dow'r, my child, and not the maid.

Flow'r of mint.
    Where true love once has been
It leaves esteem, its lasting print.

O bloom of May.
   If I discoursèd with my love an hour
That happy hour would seem the longest day.

Flow'r of broom.
   If all my sighs were flames of fire
They all the world would soon consume.

Sweet laurel bloom.
   I for a husband would a ringer choose,
That he might ring sweet peals above my tomb.

Flow'r of millet.
   Tobacco's good, and better is the box;
I think of you at least whene'er I fill it.

1875

From Dafydd ap Gwilym's 'I'r Gwynt' ('To the Wind')

Swift is the course thou runnest now,
Along the highsloped mountain's brow,
Stripping the bushes on thy track,
And answering none, by none sent back.
No leader's might, no sworded train,
No blue-steeled blade, no flood, no rain,
No fire's flame, no wily will,
No son of man can keep thee still,
No drowning depth, no warning tongue,
No hook whereon thou may'st be hung.
Thou needest no swift steed to ride,
Nor bridge nor boat where rivers glide.
No catchpole takes thee, and no clan
Repels thee, gather'd man by man.
O when thou goest forth in play

With timber'd woods along thy way,
None sees thee naked on the plain,
Though thousands hear thee, nest of rain,
Loud teazing breaker of the oak tree's bough,
A pow'r of God on earth art thou.

1875

The Cock

(After the Welsh of Siôn Powel, c. 1731–1767, in the *Hir a Thoddaid* or 'The Long and Melting Measure')

I heard the homely cock by fits to crow,
With golden wings, ere dawn began to glow,
And sing his cheery sounds from high to low,
Mild in the morn, amid the glitt'ring snow;
Sweet as the nightingale,[1] I trow, thou art.
To thy bold heart, be joy without a woe.

1876

[1] The Welsh has 'And its tune is a sweeter song than the cuckoo's'.

282

GLOSSARY

Alassen, lest.

Aller, the alder tree.

A-stooded (as of a waggon), with wheels sunk fast into soft ground.

A-stogged, with feet stuck fast in mud.

A-strout, stiff stretched.

Athirt, athwart.

Avore, before.

Axan, ashes (of fire).

Barken, a stock-yard or cow-yard.

Blooth, blossom.

Brocks, broken pieces (as of food).

Caddle, a muddle; a puzzling plight.

Clips, to clasp.

Clote, yellow water-lily.

Dather, to bewilder.

Doust, dust.

Drong, a narrow way.

Drough, through.

Durn, side post of a doorway.

Eegrass, aftermath.

Eltrot, cowparsley.

Emmet, an ant.

Emmetbut, an anthill.

Fall, autumn.

Fay, to succeed.

Frith, brushwood.

Gil'cup, buttercup (gilt cup).

Greygle, bluebell.

Hangèn, side of a hill.

Hansel, a hand gift.

Happer, to fall hopping, like hail or apples.

Hatch, a half-door.

Heft, weight.

Hele, to pour.

Ho, to be anxious.

Humstrum, a homemade musical instrument with strings.

Hayward, the warden whose duty it was to protect the right of common. He would 'drive the common', i.e. drive all the stock into a corner and impound those beasts whose owners had no right of common.

Kern, to grow into fruit.

Knap, a hillock.

283

Lawn, unploughed land.

Leäne, a lane.

Leäse, to glean.

Leäze, an unmown field, stocked through the spring and summer.

Lew, sheltered from the wind.

Lewth, lewness.

Litsome, lightsome, gay.

Litty, light and brisk of body.

Maesh, moss.

Ment, to signify.

Me'th, mirth.

Mid, might.

Mither ho, come hither. A call to a horse on the road.

Moot, the stump and roots of a felled tree.

Nesh, soft.

Nesthooden, the hooding over a nest, as a wren's.

Nitch, a load.

Nunch, luncheon.

Nut (of a wheel), the stock or nave.

Oves, eaves.

Pank, to pant.

Parrock, a small enclosed field.

Pa'sels, parcels of hay into which the **rollers** (q.v.) were scattered.

Peäviers, flag-stones.

Plim, to swell up.

Plow, a waggon (a plough for ploughing is a **zull**).

Plounce, a strong plunge.

Pooks, big peaked heaps of hay into which the drying weäles, or ridges, made up of the pa'sels, were put up when there was fear of rain.

Rathe, early.

Reäves, the ladder-like framework attached to the sides of a waggon, to uphold the load extended laterally over the wheels.

Reely, to dance a reel.

Rig, to climb in play or wantonness.

Robinhood, red campion.

Roller, in haymaking the shape into which the drying grass was first raked after being tedded and turned.

Rout, a rut.

Ruf, a roof.

Ruffen, roofing.

Scote, to shoot along.

284

Scroff, small bits of dead wood fallen under trees, or leavings under wood piles or faggots.

Shrouds, heads of trees.

Snags, small pea-big sloes.

Sneäd, a scythe stem.

Sock, a short sigh.

Spike, lavender.

Sprack, active, quick.

Spuddle, to dig slightly and incontinuously

Staddle, a bed, or a frame for ricks.

Stannên, a stall in a fair or market.

Stout, the gadfly.

Stunpoll, a stone head, blockhead.

Sumple, supple.

Tile, toil.

Tine, (i) to kindle; (ii) to fence in ground.

Tutty, a nosegay.

Tweil, see Tile.

Veät, a cheese-vat.

Vinny Cheese, cheese with blue mould.

Vuzz, Vuzzen, furze, gorse.

Wag, to stir.

Weäle, in haymaking a ridge of hay. See **pa'sel** and **pook**.

Whiver, to hover, quiver.

Whog, said to horses to make them move to the driver's right.

Widdicks, small twigs or brushwood.

Zull, a plough.

PRONUNCIATION

In the collected edition of the Dorset poems (1879) Barnes gave 'a few hints on Dorset word-shapes'. The main sounds are:

1. **ee** in beet
2. **e**, a sound between 1 and 3
3. **a** in mate
4. **i** in birth
5. **a** in father
6. **aw** in awe
7. **o** in dote
8. **oo** in rood.

In his notation:

aï, aÿ, as in maïd, Maÿ, combines 5 and 1.

eä, short as in leäd, meäd, combines 1 and 4.

eä, long as in leäde, meäde, combines 1 and 3.

ea expresses 2, as in meat.

wo, as in bwold, expresses the long o, 7.

INDEX OF TITLES

288

INDEX OF TITLES

INDEX OF TITLES

INDEX OF FIRST LINES

293